# OUTDOORS

## SIMPLE DELICIOUS FOOD FOR BARBECUES, SPITS AND OPEN FIRES

# OUTDOORS

## SIMPLE DELICIOUS FOOD FOR BARBECUES, SPITS AND OPEN FIRES

### JEREMY SCHMID

PHOTOGRAPHY BY DEVIN HART

NEW
HOLLAND

# CONTENTS

# ≡ INTRODUCTION

On the world stage New Zealand's reputation for the enjoyment of outdoor living is first class. Famous for having a great diversity of spectacular scenery it remains a popular destination for all manner of outdoor sports and recreational pursuits. The relaxed and casual lifestyle means that we enjoy socializing while eating outdoors. Depending on the occasion, "outdoors" could mean being in the mountains, by the lake, at the beach, on the back lawn, on the deck or on an apartment balcony. Many families own some kind of outdoor cooking device, but even this is not necessary to enjoy a picnic.

In our hardware stores today the range of barbecue appliances, outdoor ovens, grills and smokers can make you wish you were not restricted by budget or space or both! Gone are the days of throwing a packet of basic sausages or steak on the "barbie" with an attitude that "near enough is good enough", or "she'll be right". Nowadays, we want style, flavor and expert presentation. You just can't beat the smoky atmosphere, sizzling sounds and delicious smells of outdoor cooking as a drawcard. Of course, there remains a love of simplicity. Simplicity can be very hard to beat.

We really do like to entertain outdoors. Even changeable weather patterns won't dampen the fun of inviting friends and family over for an outdoor meal. These days we might even have durable, weatherproof, comfortable furniture and roll down transparent blinds. Rain does not stop play!

My own introduction to outdoor cooking, when I was very young, was on a very basic home-built, brick, wood-fired barbecue. It only had a flat, iron plate which we had to scrape-off and clean well each spring. It certainly demanded a lot more time and effort than a modern gas appliance. Actually, at first, we children were roped in to collect wood and clean the cooking surface, then we progressed to being able to lay out and light the fire under the plate and stoke the flames until the fire was deemed to have sufficient heat in the embers. As we mastered fire-making we watched and learned how to cook without reducing the meal to cinders. This was all about summer entertainment, fun and laughter … just as long as you positioned yourself up-wind of the initial smoke from the fire! Surely a typical snapshot of outdoor entertainment would be someone standing next to a barbecue with a long fork or tongs in one hand and a beer in the other, surrounded by a few happy "friendly helpers and advisors".

*Outdoors* complements my two previous books, *Bangers to Bacon* and *Smoked*, in that while it does incorporate some of the ideas that I've presented before, the main accent this time is on a more relaxed and uncomplicated approach so that we can enjoy food preparation and presentation in the outdoors. The recipes are grouped together in chapters depending on which ingredient has the main focus.

I've included recipe ideas that are suitable for home preparation and that you can then take on your travels at a later time. These are meals that you can perhaps take on a picnic, (which I've marked throughout as "PF" for picnic food), or meals you can take to eat with friends, adding the finishing touches to complete the dish at a different location. Some recipes can be made a day ahead and kept overnight in the refrigerator for when you have one of those "bring a plate" invitations the next day. Preparing ahead is a really effective way to limit

stress when you might be busy or at work for most of the day of the event. There are also recipes for when a cooking appliance is not available, or appropriate—for example at the races—but when a simple, attractively-prepared meal is required and needs to be presented in containers.

I feel sure you will agree there is something for everyone here. From brunches to lunches, from small get-togethers to large garden parties and special celebrations, you'll be able to find something delicious to suit the occasion.

Have fun, get cooking and enjoy the traditional way of entertaining in the great outdoors!

# ≡ COOKING EQUIPMENT AND TECHNIQUES

## BARBECUES, SPITS AND OPEN FIRES

There are many types and styles of barbecues and they are all a little different, but all of them have one thing in common—they have a heat source and some type of grill to cook your food.

### Gas barbecues

Gas barbecues are the easiest to start and use. They are very good at keeping an even temperature with little to no work and they are reliable. They come in many sizes, but getting one with a lid to form a cooking chamber will help you to expand your cooking options.

If you don't want to spend time starting and maintaining a fire this will be your best option, though you will not get that much of that sought-after smoked flavor with these units as you will with charcoal or wood.

To get a smoky flavor in your cooking you can attach a smoke generator, such as a Smokai, to the barbecue. A Smokai is a unit that produces cold smoke and it can be attached to a barbecue that has a lid. There are other units that do a similar job which may be available in your area.

For a simple, cost-effective way to get a smoke flavor you can wrap sawdust in aluminum foil and poke holes in the foil, then place it on the hot grill 4-5 minutes before you wish to start cooking and allow it to produce smoke. By closing the lid this will help flavor the foods you are cooking.

### Charcoal barbecues

Charcoal barbecues also come in a variety of sizes and styles ranging from those that look like a traditional gas barbecue, to large, egg-shaped barbecues made of ceramic.

Charcoal barbecues will give you a better flavor than gas, but they require a little more attention to maintain a constant heat, though these days some units can be very efficient and do not require a lot of attention to maintain an even temperature.

Ceramic barbecues like the Big Green Egg work really well. The thick ceramic sides insulate the unit, making it easy to achieve a constant temperature while using less fuel. They have a vent at the top to regulate the heat and allow you to get the temperature you require with relative ease.

Other charcoal barbecues look much like gas-style ones in shape and size. These tend to be less insulated and thus require a little more attention to maintain an even temperature.

There are lots of options to choose from and it's best to find a charcoal barbecue that will suit the space you have available.

### Wood barbecues

Just like charcoal barbecues, wood barbecues also come in various shapes and sizes. They will give you a smoky flavor when cooking and by using different woods you will achieve different flavors to your finished foods. They require more attention than other barbecues to start and maintain and they take longer to get a good ember base before use.

Pizza ovens can also be considered wood barbecues, and can be used to cook a lot of the foods

in this book. Pizza ovens tend to be more expensive and are usually purpose-built, but now there are many kits available and there is a lot of information around about building your own.

## Spits

Spit roasters come in two styles, horizontal or vertical. They can be either gas or solid fuel.

Both styles are great ways to cook whole animals and large joints of meat. The style that is most commonly available will most likely determine the style that you use.

Horizontal, gas-fired spits are commonly available to hire and they are a good way to start when you first try this method. They can also be bought quite cheaply these days online. Be sure to check the weight limits they are designed to hold, and that you have the correct size for the animal you intend to cook.

### Make your own spit

Spits are also very easy to make yourself. Here's how:

Buy a solid steel 1 cm (½ inch) rod around 180 cm (6 ft) in length.

Ask your local steel fabricator to make, at one end, two, 90 degree bends of about 30 cm (1 ft) each to form an "L" shape at one end. You can use this bend to use as the handle.

Drill two holes about 10 cm (4 inches) in from each end on the main shaft. You can use the holes to tie the wire you use to secure the meat onto the shaft.

Then, using large hollow concrete building bricks, build two pyramid stacks about 110–120 cm (3½–4 ft) apart and around 90 cm (3 ft) high.

Top the pyramid with a half-block to hold the rod.

### A simple horizontal spit roast

Build a fire underneath with wood and charcoal. Place the meat on the spit shaft, but away from the spit. It is important to secure the meat by either using spit skewers that pierce the meat and clamp onto the pole (preventing the animal from slipping while cooking) or by trussing very tightly with wire. Also it's important to make sure that the animal is balanced on the rod and that it's trussed so the legs are not loose and free to move while cooking.

When the fire has burned down and you have embers coated in white ash, rake the embers so that you have two lines down each side of the spit so that when the meat starts to cook the drips will not land in the fire but between the two rows of heated embers. This will help prevent flare ups which will happen if the fat drips into the fire.

Now place the meat on the spit and start cooking your meat, turning it every 10–15 minutes to ensure even cooking.

### Vertical spit roasts

Vertical spits are spits where the animal or joint is standing upright or on an angle. You see this commonly seen in kebab shops.

I use one that I had made up for me by friends at a local stainless steel fabricators, based on pictures that I had of a cross-style spit I had seen in Porteño, a restaurant in Sydney.

Vertical spits can also be made from green wood, tied with wire to secure the meat, then hammered into the ground at an angle, about 60 cm (2ft) away from the fire.

If using a wooden stake, make sure that it is tied to the skin side of the animal so that the bones are exposed to the fire during most of the cooking process to prevent the wood from burning. The bones will protect the meat during cooking.

Then finish it off by turning it over to crisp up the skin.

When making a fire scrape the embers into two piles underneath the thicker parts of the legs so when the fat drips, it does not drip into the fire.

## Cleaning and storing

Cleaning is a job no one wants, but should be done every time you use your barbecue. It's quite simple and if you maintain your equipment to the manufacturer's specifications you should have years of trouble-free cooking.

It helps to have a good wire brush, a scraper and a barbecue cover.

While the flat plate or grill grate is still warm, scrape off any food left on the grill. Use a scraper on a flat plate and a wire brush on a grill plate. This is usually enough of a clean if you are using the grill often.

To prepare the grill for long storage times, clean the grill plates in hot soapy water, rinse, dry well and lightly oil. Replace them on to the barbecue and store the unit either inside or well covered.

For gas barbecues, ensure the valve to the bottle is turned off before storage.

# FUELS

## Woods

There are many types of wood that you can use. They will give you different flavors and burn at different speeds.

There are two types of wood - hard and soft woods. Soft wood, like pine, is good to start your fire as it burns easily and quickly. After the fire is going you will need seasoned hard wood. "Seasoned" in the sense of wood for barbecues is wood that has been dried for six months or more. If you use unseasoned or green wood it will burn more slowly and cooler. To achieve a hot, slow-burning fire you will need seasoned hard woods like Manuka (tea tree), Oak, Beech, Mesquite, Cherry or Apple wood.

They are generally readily available and can be bought by the sack load.

Avoid using soft woods for the whole barbecue as they will burn too fast and not create enough heat. Another disadvantage of soft woods is that they often

have a lot of resin in them and they let off aromas that will taint the flavor of your food.

## Charcoal

Charcoal comes in two readily available forms: Briquettes and hardwood or lump charcoal.

They are both great cooking fuels and the choice depends on what you like and find easy to use.

Briquettes do a good job for most Barbecues and are lighter than lump charcoal. Essentially they are a mixture of charred wood and added binders that are pressed to form evenly-shaped pieces.

Briquettes tend to burn a little cooler and slower

than charcoal and also leave more ash to clean up. But they are easier to use than charcoal and as they are all the same size, they make it easier for you to control the temperature.

Hardwood charcoal is the most natural form of charcoal, as it's just charred hard wood left in its natural state. This is easy to see as it comes in the shapes of real wood pieces.

Hardwood charcoal will burn hotter and cleaner than briquettes and you will get a cleaner flavor. There's also less ash to clean up afterward. Because of the irregular shape it comes in and the heat it produces, it requires a little more care to maintain an even heat.

## Gas

Gas is the easiest fuel type to use. It's easy to start and it's easy to maintain a consistent heat. One 20 lb (9kg) gas bottle will give you many happy hours on the barbecue. The disadvantage of gas is that you will not get the distinctive flavor that you would by using wood or charcoal.

Keep the jets clean where the gas burns, as some barbecues do not have protection from the drips that fall off as the food cooks.

Make sure there is sufficient gas for the duration of your cooking. There's nothing worse than running out of gas when the barbecue is only half cooked!

# BRINING AND SMOKING TECHNIQUES

The more you get into barbecuing the more likely you are to want to try smoking your meats and vegetables. Here are some basic ideas and techniques to get you started:

## Smoking

When smoking on your barbecue you have a few different options to choose from.

You can use a stovetop smoker and place this directly onto the grill plate for your barbecue to get the heat from below to smoke.

You can find units like a Smokai or something similar that can be mounted to most barbecue lids to produce cold smoke. A Smokai can be used when you are cooking on the barbecue in order to add flavor to your meats, vegetables and occasionally even fruit! When you have these types of units you can also use the chamber of your barbecue to cold-smoke foods. This makes for a very versatile barbecue!

As I mentioned earlier, another way to smoke your food is to wrap fine wood chips in foil, pick the foil with a knife or skewer, then place this on to the grill plate and wait until the chips start smouldering to create smoke. Then you can start to cook your food. You will need a barbecue with a lid to get the best results.

If you are using a charcoal-fuelled barbecue you can throw soaked wood chips onto the charcoal while you are cooking. The chips will smoulder to flavor the food.

Different varieties of woods will give you different flavors.

## Wood flavor profiles

FRUIT WOODS: Sweet, light, pleasant by themselves or can be blended with stronger woods. Fruit woods include apple, cherry and pear.

HICKORY: Strong and good by itself or can also be blended with fruit woods.

MANUKA (TEA TREE): Strong and heavy. Blends well with fruit woods.

OAK: Strong, though not overpowering. Good by itself or blended with maple.

MESQUITE: Very strong by itself and good to blend with maple or fruit woods.

MAPLE: A sweet, good, stand-alone wood. Use like fruit woods.

WALNUT: A strong wood that is best blended with lighter woods

## Brining

When hot-smoking meats, they should be brined before smoking. This will help with the taste and tenderness.

As with any brining process it is best to bring the brine to a boil and then fully cool it down before adding the meats. You can use the brining method for many different cuts of meats including any whole birds that you wish to smoke. You can add flavor to the meats by adding different ingredients to the brines.

The size of the meat to be brined will make a difference to the brining time, and a brine pump will speed up the process.

## Meat injection and brine pumping

A meat injector is a large syringe with a thick needle used to disperse the brine when injecting it into the cut of meat when smoking or marinating it. Smaller syringe-type injectors are suitable for pieces of bacon, chicken or any smaller cuts where you wish to inject brine or marinade.

A brine pump is used for brining large cuts of meat, such as a whole pork leg, allowing the brine to get close to the bone and spread throughout all the meat, speeding up the brining process.

The "working end" of the brine pump is the injector needle. As a simple rule of thumb, if the injector needle can reach the middle of the meat from both sides it should be long enough to brine or marinate the meat correctly.

Brine pumps and injector needles can be

Basic guidelines for brining times:

| Meat cut | Unpumped | Pumped |
|---|---|---|
| Whole chicken (size 18-20; 1.8-2kg) | 4 days | 24 hours |
| Chicken or duck breast (200-250 g) | 2 days | 12 hours |
| Pork leg (whole) (6-7kg) | 28 days | 7 days |
| Pork belly whole (3-4kg) | 5 days | 2 days |
| Venison loin (500 g) | 4 days | 24 hours |
| Beef brisket (1 kg) | 7 days | 2 days |

purchased from butchery suppliers or specialist barbecue shops. Some marinades are supplied with a basic pump or injector that can be reused.

## The meat thermometer

A meat thermometer comes in handy when you need to know the final internal temperature of a cooked or smoked product. They are especially useful for long, slow cooking processes.

I find them really useful because it does not matter how long you have been cooking, you can never get a true indication of the internal temperature of the meat without one. I use mine all the time for many cooking processes.

You can get a couple of different types.

In a remote thermometer, the probe and the temperature display are separated via a cable. This allows you to have the probe in the item you are cooking with the lid on and you can see the temperature without having to lift the lid every time.

The other type of thermometer is a simple handheld digital thermometer. I use this type often as I usually check different places of the meat and it's also fast to check multiple pieces quickly.

They are not expensive and a great tool to have when barbecuing or smoking food.

## Grill brush

When cooking on a barbecue it's good to have a long-handled grill brush. These come in all shapes and sizes. Get one that is appropriate for your barbecue and use it to make sure the grill plates are always cleaned after use.

## Fire extinguisher

It's a good idea when having an open fire to have one of these handy. Have an all purpose unit that is charged and serviced annually.

## Other things that you will need

You will need a selection of chopping boards; good, sharp knives and plastic containers with tight-fitting lids that fit into your refrigerator.

You will also need a set of digital scales, a strainer, natural string, cling wrap, a measuring jug and spoons, aluminum foil, kitchen scissors, tongs, scrapers and other general kitchen equipment.

# BEEF
# &
# LAMB

# » SMOKED, SLOW-COOKED BRISKET (PF)

Smoky brisket is a great dish to take to any picnic or gathering. It will feed a few people and once cooked can stay warm for a few hours if you wrap it in aluminum foil and place in an ice chest filled with crumpled newspaper. It takes time to make but the results are worth the effort.

## INGREDIENTS
1 flat cut brisket about 6½ lb (3 kg)
6 tablespoons beef rub #2 (page 195)

### Injection mixture
8 fl oz (250 ml) beef stock
¾ fl oz (20 ml) Worcestershire sauce
1 teaspoon smoked paprika
½ teaspoon garlic powder

**Serves 8–10**

## METHOD
Remove brisket from packaging and pat it dry with paper towels and prepare your cold smoker with 7 oz (200 g) of chips for a one hour smoke.

Add the brisket to the cold smoker and smoke the brisket for 1 hour. I like to use oak or hickory, but the choice is yours.

In a medium size bowl, mix all of the ingredients for the injection mixture together until combined. Set aside.

After the cold smoke is complete, remove the brisket and wrap it in plastic wrap and evenly inject the mix into the brisket using a meat injector.

Inject all the liquid then unwrap the brisket and pat dry with paper towel.

Preheat the barbecue to 230°F (110°C).

Season the brisket with the rub mix and place the brisket fat side down into a medium sided baking tray with a cake rack in the base. Cook for 3 hours.

After 3 hours, remove the brisket and wrap it in aluminum foil and return to cook, fat side up, for 2 hours or until the internal temperature reaches 185-195°F (85-90°C).

Remove from the barbecue and rest for 20 minutes before serving.

# » BARBECUE BEEF SHORT RIBS

Sticky, meaty ribs are great. They take a little time to cook but are well worth the effort. Because they are so rich, I like to serve them with a vinaigrette-based potato salad and fresh salad leaves.

## INGREDIENTS
2 short beef rib racks
6 tablespoons rub #2 (see page 195
8 fl oz (250 ml) barbecue sauce (see page 184)

Serves 5–6

## METHOD
Trim the ribs of any excess fat and remove the membrane from the bone side of the ribs.

Season the ribs with beef rub #2 using 2/3 on the meat side and 1/3 on the bone side. Place on an oven tray and stand for 30 minutes.

Preheat the barbecue using non-direct heat to 230–250°F (110–120°C)

Place the ribs in the barbecue and cook for 2 hours.

Remove the ribs from the barbecue and place each of the slabs onto a large sheet of aluminum foil. Brush the ribs with 2/3 of the barbecue sauce and lightly wrap them in the foil to allow steam to be released during the cooking process.

Place the 2 packets of foil-wrapped ribs back into the barbecue and cook for a further 2 hours or until tender.

To check for tenderness poke the sharp end of a bamboo skewer into the meat. There should be little resistance. If necessary return to the barbecue until done to your satisfaction.

Once fully cooked, remove the ribs from the barbecue and increase the barbecue temperature to 325°F (170°C).

Unwrap the ribs, place them onto a tray and brush them with the remaining barbecue sauce before returning them to barbecue for another 10-15 minutes until brown and caramelized - making the ribs sticky and extra tasty.

# »BEEF SCOTCH RIB ROTISSERIE ROAST

This is the king of roasts. Also known as the bone-in rib eye steak, or the côte de bœuf, they cook equally well in a barbecue but I really like the results on the spit. They are large so will feed a few people, even the big eaters. And being able to chew on the bone is really satisfying after the long cooking time.

## INGREDIENTS
1 beef scotch OP rib 6½-8½ lbs (3-4 kg)
10 garlic cloves
10 fl oz (300 ml) salt water glaze (page 194)
salt and freshly-ground black pepper

Serves 6–8

## METHOD
Preheat the gas barbecue with a rotisserie attachment to around 230–250°F (110–120°C).

Using a small knife, make a small incision in the beef and insert a piece of garlic and repeat this process until all the garlic is inserted into the beef. Try to evenly space the garlic throughout the meat, keeping it within ¾ inch (2 cm) of the surface.

Season the beef well before inserting the spit rod through the middle of the beef, securing both ends with spit clamps or wire.

Place the meat onto the spit and roast, basting with the salt glaze every 30 minutes until you achieve an internal temperature of 125-30°F (52-55°C). Roast for 1 to 1.5 hours depending on whether you want the meat medium rare or medium.

Allow to stand 10-15 minutes before carving.

# » BEEF PATTIES

These patties taste great in burgers but this mix is versatile enough to be used in sausage rolls or made into meatballs. So you can always make more than you need and use the extra for tomorrow's dinner.

## INGREDIENTS

2¼ lb (1 kg) beef chuck including the fat cap, cut into 1 inch (3 cm) cubes
2 teaspoon fine salt salt
½ teaspoon ground black pepper
1 teaspoon raw sugar
3 tablespoons tomato sauce
2 garlic cloves, crushed
1 tablespoon smoked paprika
2¾ fl oz (80 ml) dark ale
2 tablespoons rice flour
1 tablespoon whole grain mustard
canola oil, for cooking

**Serves 4–6**

## METHOD

In a large bowl mix all the ingredients together, cover with plastic wrap and marinate overnight.

The next day, mince the beef on a medium plate using your hand or a paddle attachment on your food mixer to mix the mince together well.

Form the beef mixture into 6 patties.

To cook, heat the barbecue to a medium heat and add a little oil.

Fry the patties on one side for around 3-4 minutes then turn them over and fry for 3-4 minutes longer, or until just cooked. Try to avoid pressing them down with your turning utensil as you want them to retain as much moisture as possible.

Once cooked, let the patties rest for a minute or two before serving.

# »BEEF BURGERS

We all love a great burger and making your own patties gives you the option to add the flavors you like. If you don't like a lot of garlic, leave it out. If you really like onions, add some more. This is a chance to experiment a little and to make your perfect patty.

## INGREDIENTS

6 burger buns, cut in half
6 tablespoons tomato chutney
   (see page 185)
½ iceberg lettuce, finely sliced
2 large tomatoes, sliced
6 beef patties (see page 26 for
   recipe)
12 slices of cheese
1 small red onion, finely sliced
   into rings
6 tablespoons aioli

Serves 6

## METHOD

To assemble the burgers, warm the buns in the barbecue for a minute or two.

On each bottom bun, first add a tablespoon of tomato chutney, then top with lettuce, tomato, the beef patty, two slices of cheese, some red onion then add the aioli to the top half of the bun to complete the burger.

Serve warm.

# » GRILLED SIRLOIN "DOUBLE STEAK"

I like these extra thick sirloins. Unless you like a large portion, they are good for two people and are best carved after cooking. Best served medium with a thin layer of the fat cap removed. They grill beautifully.

## INGREDIENTS

2 double sirloins 17½-21 oz
  (500–600 g) each
2 cloves garlic
1 sprig rosemary, picked
2½ fl oz (75 ml) canola oil
salt and freshly-cracked pepper

**Serves 4**

## METHOD

In a high-speed blender, blend the garlic, rosemary and the oil and add some salt and pepper.

Place the oil into a zip-lock plastic bag or container large enough to hold the sirloin.

Place the sirloin into the oil marinade and marinate for 2-6 hours or overnight.

Remove the sirloin from the oil and allow to warm to room temperature on a plate.

Heat the barbecue grill plate to low or medium heat.

Place the steaks onto the barbecue and cook for around 4 minutes on each of the four sides, then repeat the process for a cooking time of around 32–38 minutes to achieve an internal temperature of 125-130°F (52-54°C).

Rest for 5 minutes and carve.

Serve warm.

# » BEEF T-BONE, CAFÉ DE PARIS BUTTER AND JACKET POTATOES

Cooking a T-bone can be a little more difficult than other cuts without a bone as the meat around the bone will take longer to cook due to the bone, which insulates the meat from the heat source.

## INGREDIENTS

4 T-bone steaks 16–17½ oz (450–500 g) each, 2 inches (5 cm) thick
4 potatoes, 7 oz (200 g) each, skin on
3½ oz (100 g) sour cream
2 tablespoons chives, finely chopped
4½ oz (120 g) Café de Paris butter (page 182)
canola oil, for cooking
salt and freshly-ground black pepper

**Serves 4**

## METHOD

Preheat the barbecue to 325°F (170°C).

Wrap the potatoes in aluminum foil and put them on the barbecue on an indirect heat.

Cook the potatoes for 1 hour or until soft. To test this, use a skewer and pierce the potato, if there is no resistance they are done. Once cooked, remove them from the barbecue and let cool for 10 minutes.

Allow the T-bone steak to get up to room temperature while cooking the potatoes.

When the potatoes are cooked, prepare the steak.

Lightly oil them and season the steak liberally with salt and pepper before placing them onto the grill of the barbecue.

Cook for 6-7 minutes on each side or until the internal temperature closest to the bone reaches 130°F (54-56°C).

Allow to rest for 4-5 minutes.

To serve, remove the aluminum from the potatoes, cut a cross in the top of the potato cutting 1/3 of the way through. With your fingers, press each potato on the sides inwards in such a way that the middle of the potato is exposed.

Top the potato with sour cream, chives and salt and pepper.

Top the T-bone with Café de Paris butter. Season with freshly-cracked pepper and serve warm.

# »LAMB KOFTA (PF)

For this recipe I like to marinate the meat overnight then mince the following day. If you don't have a mincer, buy lean lamb mince to cut down the time on this process. By marinating it overnight, you will find that the kofta mix binds together well and the flavors develop nicely.

## INGREDIENTS

2½ lbs (1 kg) lamb trim or lamb shoulder diced into 1–1.5 inch (3–4 cm) cubes
½ tablespoon fine salt
1 teaspoon raw sugar
½ teaspoon ground black pepper
1 tablespoon mustard whole grain
1 teaspoon cumin ground
3 garlic cloves, minced
1½ teaspoon ground coriander
1 tablespoon fresh coriander leaves, coarsely cut
8 metal skewers

**Serves 8**

## METHOD

In a large bowl mix all the ingredients (except for the fresh coriander) then cover with plastic wrap and chill overnight.

Using a fine plate on the mincer, mince the meat and add the coriander. Then, using your hands, mix the meat together until well bound.

Divide into 3 oz (60-70 g) portions and form into a ball, then roll gently on a chopping board to create an oval shape.

Thread the balls onto metal skewers so each skewer has two pieces on each skewer.

Preheat the barbecue at a low to medium heat.

Cook the koftas for about 7-10 minutes, turning occasionally. The length of cooking will vary depending on their thickness.

Once cooked, rest for a few minutes and serve hot.

Serve with yogurt dressing and couscous.

# » GARLIC & ROSEMARY STUDDED LAMB LEG

We all like a good roast and doing this on the barbecue not only gives you great flavor, but it is a real show stopper when serving. Carving a beautifully cooked lamb leg is always impressive and allows you to entertain with minimal work.

## INGREDIENTS
4 1/2 lb (2kg) lamb leg
6 garlic cloves cut in half
  lengthwise
1 sprig rosemary
salt and pepper

Serves 6–8

## METHOD
Using a barbecue with a lid, preheat it to 265°F (135°C)

Place the lamb leg skin side down and use a small knife to make a small incision in the lamb and insert a piece of garlic and some of the rosemary. Repeat until all the garlic is inserted.

Liberally season the lamb with salt and pepper then place it on a cake rack with a low sided tray underneath. Pour one cup of water into the tray. The water may need to be topped up during cooking so check this every 30-40 mintes.

Place the tray into the barbecue and cover with the lid. Cook the meat for 2.5 to 3 hours or until the internal temperature reaches 70°C (155°F). Then, turn up the heat to 400°F (200°C) for 10 minutes or so until the leg is golden brown.

Remove from the barbecue and rest the meat for 10-15 minutes before carving.

# »WHOLE LAMB SPIT

Roasting whole beasts must be the most rewarding forming of cooking. When cooking using an open fire you will need to be careful where you do it and it will take some time. You will also need to ensure you keep the fire at an even temperature by always adding a little wood or charcoal to the fire. The last thing you want to happen is for the fire to go out!

## INGREDIENTS
1 whole lamb 33–38 lb
  (15–17kg)
1 quart (1 liter) salt water glaze
  (see page 194)
canola oil, for cooking
salt

**Serves 20+**

## METHOD

It's a good idea to have a helper when cooking this as dealing with a whole lamb is sometimes difficult and an extra pair of hands make things easier.

Using a meat saw or large meat cleaver, cut the lamb through the middle of the chest and between the hind legs so that it opens up.

Lightly oil the lamb and season with salt.

Tie the lamb to the bars of the cross with wire, ensuring that it is secure and will not fall off during the cooking process. I like to cook it upside down as the hind legs are thicker and will be over the heat more when cooking if it's secured this way. You can easily use some green wood for this as it's far enough away from the heat not to combust.

While you get the fire ready, take out your lamb from the refrigerator. Ideally you want to start cooking it when at room temperature because the whole process slows down if the lamb is too cold.

When you have burned down the wood to embers or when the charcoal has a white haze then put the lamb around 24 inches (60 cm) away and at a 15° angle to the fire.

Start cooking the lamb bone side first, as the bones will help protect the meat while cooking.

Spread the embers or charcoal so that they are built up under the hind

recipe continues »

recipe continues **»**

legs rather than the middle as the heat will radiate and when the fat drips it will drip more in the middle where you will have less fire.

When cooking the lamb I flip it over periodically - around 40 minutes on the bone side then 20 minutes on the skin side and so on.

Baste the lamb once an hour with the salt glaze.

When the juices are flowing from the lamb or when the hind leg temperature is (165°F) 75°C , or both, turn the lamb to the skin side and crisp up the skin before removing from the heat.

Place the cooked lamb onto a large table, remove the wooden cross and rest for 10 minutes before carving to serve.

# »LAMB HIND SHANKS SLOW ROASTED WITH APRICOT, THYME AND CARDAMOM CHUTNEY

Lamb shanks are high on the list of cuts I enjoy cooking and eating. Often they are braised but slow-roasting is an excellent way to enjoy them. The chutney will work well with other lamb dishes as well as with chicken.

## INGREDIENTS
4 lamb hind shanks
1 sprig rosemary, roughly chopped
4 garlic cloves, minced
2 fl oz (50 ml) canola oil
salt and freshly-ground black pepper

### Apricot, thyme and cardamom chutney
2½ lb (1 kg) apricots, pitted and halved
17½ oz (500 g) onions, diced
9 oz (250 g) raisins
14 oz (400 g) brown sugar
12½ oz (350 ml) cider vinegar
2 teaspoons mustards seeds
5–6 sprigs fresh thyme
10 cardamom pods, crushed
1 teaspoon salt

Serves 4

## METHOD
Preheat a lidded barbecue to 265°F (130°C).

Mix the rosemary, garlic, oil and salt and pepper together, rub this on to the shanks, place the shanks onto a cake rack in the base of the tray.

Pour in 8 fl oz (250 ml) of water into the tray and place the whole tray onto the barbecue, cover with the lid and slowly roast for 3 hours or until the meat is tender to touch or 185°F (85°C) internal temperature. The water may need to be topped up during cooking, check this every 30 minutes or so.

Remove from the barbecue and rest for 5-10 minutes before serving.

To make the chutney, place in all the ingredients in a large saucepan and over a medium to high heat bring to a boil.

Reduce the heat to a gentle simmer and cook for 1 hour, stirring every 5 minutes or so until the chutney thickens.

Pour into a clean container or jars and store in the refrigerator once cooled. The chutney will keep for 4-5 weeks.

# » LAMB CHOPS WITH MINT SAUCE

Lamb and mint is a classic combination and this mint sauce is quick to make and tasty. Chops cook quite fast so this is an easy meal to prepare and cook when time is short. It's always best to have a few extra chops because for some three is just not enough!

## INGREDIENTS

12–15 lamb chops 1 inch (2–2.5 cm) think
salt and freshly-ground black pepper
canola oil, for cooking
5 fl oz (150 ml) mint sauce (page 186)

**Serves 4**

## METHOD

Preheat the grill plate of the barbecue to medium-high heat.

Lightly oil the chops and season well with the salt and pepper.

Place the chops onto the grill plate and cook for 2-3 minutes.

Then, turn the chop on a 45° angle and cook a further 2 minutes. Repeat the process on the other side, the internal temperature should reach 130-140°F (55-60°C)

Allow to rest for a few minutes before serving with mint sauce.

# »WHOLE LAMB SHOULDER
## (PF)

This is another great dish to feed a few people at once, slowly cooked until it just falls off the bone, this dish is perfect served with crusty bread, salad and chutney. You can stud the shoulder with garlic for a different option.

## INGREDIENTS
1 lamb shoulder, whole
   4 ½–5½ lb (2–2.5kg)
2 large onions, each peeled and
   sliced into 4 quarters
2 sprigs of thyme
1 bay leaf
2 rosemary sprigs
1 garlic head, sliced in half
16 fl oz (500 ml) beef stock
3 tablespoons lamb rub #1
salt and freshly-ground black
   pepper

Serves 8–10

## METHOD
Preheat the barbecue to 350°F (180°C).

Sprinkle the rub over the lamb and let it stand for 20 minutes.

Place the onions, garlic, herbs, and stock into a high-sided tray.

Place the lamb on the tray so that it rests on the onions and put the tray into the barbecue and close the lid. Turn down the barbecue to 285°F (140°C).

Cook for 30 minutes, then remove and cover the tray with a layer of baking paper. Tightly seal the tray with aluminum foil and return to the barbecue for 2.5-3 hours or until the internal temperature reaches 175°F (80°C).

Remove the tray from the barbecue and let it stand for 20 minutes before serving.

To transport the cooked lamb shoulder, wrap well in foil and place the meat in the center of an esky filled with scrunched up newspaper. It should keep warm for an hour or so.

To serve, use a fork to break of lamb, season if necessary with salt and pepper.

# » DEBONED & BUTTERFLIED LAMB SHOULDER

When cooking a boned-out shoulder you will find it shrinks a little more than an non-boned one. It will also cook much quicker and, having more surface area to cook, it will have a lot of flavor compared to a non-boned shoulder. It's best to ask for this cut from your butcher as they will keep it in one piece.

## INGREDIENTS
1 lamb shoulder boned and
  butterflied 2¼–2½ lb (1–1.2kg)
5 tablespoons lamb rub #2
  (page 200)
canola oil, for cooking

**Serves 4–6**

## METHOD
Preheat the barbecue to 285°F (140°C).

Allow the lamb to come up to room temperature, then lightly oil the lamb and season with the rub on both sides.

Place the lamb onto the flat grill plate and cook for 10 minutes then turn over, repeating the process every 10 minutes for 50 minutes, cooking for a total of 60 minutes or until the internal temperature reached 140°F (60°C).

Once cooked allow to rest for 10 minutes before carving.

Slice into pieces and serve hot.

PORK
&
VENISON

# »PORK & BEER BURGER PATTIES

Pork and beer are great ingredients and together they make a great team for any barbecue. To make this recipe easier you can buy pork mince, but I like to marinate it overnight and mince it. But if you don't have the time to marinate overnight, don't let that stop you from trying them anyway.

## INGREDIENTS

24½ oz (700 g) pork shoulder
  cut into 2 inch (5 cm) cubes
1 teaspoon flaky salt
1 teaspoon smoked paprika
¼ teaspoon freshly ground
  black pepper
2 fl oz (60 ml) your favorite beer
3 tablespoons barbecue sauce
  (page 184)
1 teaspoon raw sugar
¼ teaspoon ground fennel
¼ teaspoon sage, dried
canola oil, for cooking

**Makes 4–6 patties**

## METHOD

In a large bowl, mix together all the ingredients until well combined. Then cover the bowl with plastic wrap and marinate contents overnight in the refrigerator.

Mince the pork on a medium plate, and mix the mince to bind. This should take around a minute or so.

Form the meat into patties. Make them as large as you need, though this will depend on the size of your buns. The patties should be around ½-¾ inch (1.5-2 cm) thick.

Preheat the barbecue flat plate to a medium heat, then add a little oil and cook the patties for 3-4 minutes on each side depending on how thick you have made them.

They should be juicy and slightly pink in the middle when finished.

Allow them to rest for a few minutes and serve separately or between some good burger buns.

# » VIETNAMESE-STYLE PORK SKEWER BAGUETTES (PF)

These Banh Mi sandwiches are very tasty with the fresh herbs and pickled vegetable slaw. If taking them to a picnic, cook the meat and make up the pickles but only put them together just before serving to make sure the buns don't become soggy. They can be spiced up with some fresh chili and scallions if desired.

## INGREDIENTS
10½ oz (300 g) trimmed pork loin cut into ¼ inch (½ cm) thin slices
4 french baguettes 10 inch (25 cm) long
8 wooden skewers 4½ inch (12 cm) long and soaked in water for 1 hour

## Meat marinade
2 garlic cloves, crushed
1 tablespoon lemongrass, white part only, finely chopped
1 tablespoon fish sauce
3 tablespoon cooking oil
1 tablespoon palm sugar

## METHOD
For the meat marinade, mix all the ingredients together in a medium size bowl.

Once combined, add in the pork and gently mix together to coat the all the pork pieces. Cover with plastic wrap and allow to marinade for a further 2 hours in the refrigerator.

Place the pork evenly onto the 8 skewers and preheat the barbecue grill to medium-high heat.

Lightly oil the skewers and place them onto the grill. Allow a cooking time of 2–3 minutes for each side. To check if cooked cut on a piece and check if they are done. If the pieces are slightly pink in the middle, they are cooked.

recipe continues »

recipe continues»

## Pickled vegetable slaw

2fl oz (60 ml) water
3 tablespoons sugar
2 tablespoons white vinegar
3½ oz (100 g) grated carrots
3½ oz (100 g) finely sliced
  daikon (giant white radish)
1 tablespoon coriander leaves
1 tablespoon vietnamese mint
  leaves
3½ oz (100 g) cucumber, finely
  sliced

## Dressing
3 oz (80 g) mayonnaise
salt and freshly-cracked pepper

**Serves 4**

To make the pickled slaw, bring the water, sugar and vinegar to a boil and cool, add the carrots and daikon and marinate for 1 hour. Then, drain and mix in the herbs and set aside.

## ASSEMBLY

Cut the buns lengthways ¾ of the way through, then open them up and spread on the mayonnaise evenly.

Place on the cucumber slices, two skewers of pork, add the pickled slaw and season with salt and pepper.

Hold the bun and carefully remove the wooden skewer leaving the meat in the bun then serve.

# »PULLED PORK SHOULDER (PF)

Pulled pork is very versatile. It can be used in sliders, quesadas, turned into a pie, Cornish pasties, or even used on a pizza. So when you cook pulled pork there is never a problem with leftovers as you are bound to find a use for it – with excellent results.

## INGREDIENTS
6¾ lb (3 kg) pork shoulder with the skin on and the bone in

**Pork rub**
4 tablespoons brown sugar
3 tablespoons salt
1 tablespoon coriander
1 tablespoon garlic powder
1 tablespoon paprika
1 tablespoon ground fennel

## METHOD
Preheat the barbecue to 260-280°F (130-140°C).

Place the pork shoulder into a large tray with high sides.

Mix all the dry ingredients together and rub onto the pork, use rubber gloves to prevent it sticking to your hands.

Add around ½ inch (1 cm) of water into the tray. Place a sheet of baking paper onto the pork then cover and seal the whole tray with aluminum foil.

Place the whole tray into the barbecue for 4 hours. After this time remove the foil and paper and return to the barbecue for a further hour or until you are able to shred the pork with a fork.

Once cooked, allow the pork to rest for 30 minutes then remove the skin and set it aside.

Use two forks to pull the pork apart and mix it in with some of the cooking juices. Season if necessary and serve warm.

**Serves 10–12**

# »ASIAN PORK SCOTCH FILLET

This is an easy and tasty recipe for an Asian-style barbecue that can be served with garlic green beans or a simple salad. If you would like to speed up the marinating process try cutting the loin into 4 portions before marinating. You can get away with 1–2 hours of marinating and still have great results.

## INGREDIENTS
1 pork scotch fillet 2¼ lb (1 kg)

### Marinade
2 tablespoons soy sauce
4 tablespoons brown sugar
3 cloves crushed garlic
½ teaspoon Chinese five spice
2 tablespoonssesame oil
10 fl oz (300 ml) water

**Serves 4**

## METHOD
Place the pork into a large zip-lock bag and set aside.

In a medium size bowl mix all the marinade ingredients together then add them into the bag with the pork. Try to remove as much air as possible from the bag before putting the bag in the refrigerator to allow the mixture to marinate for from 4 to 24 hours.

Preheat a barbecue with a lid to 300°F (150°C).

Remove the pork scotch fillet from the marinade and pat dry with paper towels. Lightly oil the pork, then place into a low-sided tray and then place into the barbecue on an indirect heat.

Cook for 20 minutes then turn and repeat this every 20 minutes for 70–80 minutes or until the internal temperatures reach 145-155°F (62–68°C).

Allow to rest to 5-10 minutes, then carve to serve.

# » WHOLE SPIT ROAST PIG

The sight of a whole animal cooking is always something of a wonder. We don't get to see this as much today as we did in the past but as with all things, whole-roast cooking is becoming popular again. Instructions for cooking with a spit are included on page 11 and spit units are readily available for hire.

## INGREDIENTS
1 whole suckling pig, 44–55 lb (20–25 kg)
salt
16 fl oz (500 ml) salt water glaze (page 194) in a plastic squirt bottle

Serves 30–40

## METHOD
If you are using a wood burning or charcoal one, start your fire long in advance as the fire will take an hour or two to get to the right temperature. If you are using a gas-fired unit start this just after you place the pig on the spit.

Before placing the animal on the spit, season the inside of its belly cavity with salt. Then, using a piece of wire, truss up the belly cavity. This will help with the even cooking of the meat.

Lay the pig on one side then push through the rod you will be using from the tail end in, through the body cavity and then out through the mouth.

Secure the pig to the rod using the spit fork on each end of the pig. Tie the front legs to the front forks using a 24-28in (60-70cm) piece of wire, as they are too short to tie to the central rod. Tie the hind legs to the rod by wrapping the center of a 24-28in (60-70cm) piece of wire around the rod a few times, then pull the hind legs as close to the rod as possible and tie them ecurely to prevent the animal from slipping while turning.

Cut off or wrap the ears in aluminum foil to prevent them from burning.

Season well with salt by rubbing it on the skin vigorously.

Place the pig over the fire or on the gas spit for around 5.5-6.5 hours. If you have a motorized unit start this now and slowly cook for around 5-6 hours or until you have an internal temperature of 160-165°F (72-75°C). If you have to hand-crank the spit, rotate the pig every 5-10 minutes a quarter turn.

**recipe continues »**

To baste the pig, start squeezing the glaze over the pig around 4-5 hours into the cooking, then every 30 minutes after that. If you find the skin is getting too dark, lift the pig higher in the spit or cover it with foil.

Once cooked, carefully remove the pig and let it rest for 15-20 minutes.

Carve the pig by removing the hind legs first and then the forelegs before carving the middle section.

# »PORK BELLY SLIDERS (PF)

When cooking the belly for the sliders you will need a barbecue with a lid and for the best results preferably one using charcoal or wood to get some tasty smoke flavor into the belly. Any leftovers can be reheated for the following day if they are stored correctly and they go well in sandwiches or stir-fries. Sliders can be made beforehand and taken to a picnic in place of sandwiches. They are a real hit with kids!

## INGREDIENTS
21 oz (600 g)pork belly, sliced
2 fl oz. (60 ml) barbecue sauce
  (page 184)
12 slider buns

## Belly
1 pork belly 6 ¾ pounds (3kg) ,
  with the skin on
3 onions, peeled and coarsely
  sliced
3 carrots, roughly sliced
3 celery sticks, roughly sliced
1 bottle of your favorite beer –
  11 fl oz. (330 ml)
8 fl oz. (250 ml)water
1¾ oz. (50 g) beef rub #2
salt and freshly-ground black
  pepper
canola oil, for cooking

## METHOD
Preheat the barbecue to 300–325°F (150–160°C).

In a large, deep-sided tray place in all the vegetables and mix in the beer and water.

With a sharp knife score the skin of the pork belly, cutting 1/4 of the way through into the belly.

On the underside, rub on the beef rub and then place the meat onto the vegetables. Brush the meat with some oil and season well with salt and pepper, rubbing well into the score lines.

Place the whole tray into the barbecue and cover with the lid.

Maintain the heat between 300–325°F (150–160°C) for 3 –3.5 hours.

Once cooked the skin should be deep brown and crispy. Remove from the tray and allow to stand for 10 minutes before carving.

To make the slaw, mix all ingredients together in a large bowl until well combined. Season well to taste.

recipe continues »

recipe continues »

## Slaw

½ green cabbage, finely sliced
¼ red cabbage, finely sliced
1 red onion, finely sliced
2 carrots, peeled and grated
2 tablespoons parsley, finely
  chopped
6 tablespoons aioli
1 tablespoon balsamic vinegar
salt and freshly-ground pepper

**Serves 4–6**

## Assembly

Cut the slider buns in halves.

Spread some barbecue sauce on each bun top.

Place some slaw on the base and top with a handful of sliced pork belly, and add the top of each bun.

# »PORK CHOPS WITH APPLE & SAGE GLAZE

Chops and barbecues go hand-in-hand. They don't require a lot of preparation beforehand, which makes them convenient when you are lacking time. This basting glaze will work well with other cuts of pork too like fillet, loin or scotch fillet.

## INGREDIENTS
4 pork chops 10½ oz (300 g) each, 1¼ inch (3 cm) thick
canola oil, for cooking
salt and freshly-ground black pepper

### Basting glaze
¼ teaspoon dried sage
1 tablespoon honey
2 fl oz (60 ml) apple juice
1 pinch of cinnamon

**Serves 4**

## METHOD
Preheat the barbecue to a medium heat.

Lightly oil the pork chops and season well, then place onto the barbecue grill plate and cook for 3-4 minutes on one side, turn over and baste the cooked side. After another 3-4 minutes repeat the process. Repeat the process every 2 minutes until cooked to an internal temperature of 150°F (65°C).

Allow to rest for 5 minutes and serve hot with tomato chutney (see page 185).

# » BARBECUE PORK SPARE RIBS

If you are using a charcoal or wood barbecue you can achieve a better flavor for this dish. If you are using a gas barbecue try wrapping some sawdust or smoking chips in foil, pierce the foil and place over the grill to heat and combust causing smoke which will help flavor the ribs.

## INGREDIENTS
2 whole pork rib slabs
7 fl oz (200 ml) barbecue sauce (see page 184)
4 fl oz (120 ml) rub #2 (page 195)

Serves 4–6

## METHOD
About 20 minutes before cooking rub the ribs with beef rub #2 on both sides.

Preheat a barbecue with a lid to 275°F (135°C).

Place a cake rack onto a tray, put the ribs meat side down onto the rack and put the tray into the barbecue.

Cook for 2.5 hours and then turn over and cook a further hour or until a skewer can easily pierce through the meat with little resistance.

Remove the tray and heat the barbecue to 350°F (180°C).

Brush the ribs with the barbecue sauce and return to the barbecue for 10-15 minutes until the ribs start to caramelise.

Remove from the barbecue and let stand for 10 minutes.

Slice between the ribs and serve hot.

# »PORK & RABBIT TERRINE
## (PF)

This is a great recipe for any picnic. I make terrines often and usually have them on my menus. This one can be made a few days beforehand thus freeing up time on the day of the picnic if you need it.

## INGREDIENTS

2 ¼ lb (1 kg) pork shoulder diced into 1½ inch (4 cm) cubes
12½ oz (350 g) pork fat, diced in 1½ inch (4 cm) cubes

### Seasoning mix

1 teaspoon salt
¼ teaspoon ground pepper
¼ teaspoonground fennel
¼ teaspoon ground coriander
1 pinch dried thyme
¾ fl oz (20 ml) cognac
¾ fl oz (20 ml) dark rum

### Terrine mix

1 large onion, finely diced
⅓ oz (10 g) dried mushrooms, soaked for 20 minutes in cold water
⅓ oz (10 g) freshly crushed garlic
8 fl oz (260 ml) light cream
1 rabbit, deboned and diced into 1 ¼ – 1 ½ inch (3–4 cm) cubes
5½ oz (160 g) pork shoulder diced in 1 ¼–1 ½ inch (3–4 cm) cubes

**SERVES 8–10**

## METHOD

In a large bowl marinate the pork shoulder, pork fat, and seasoning mix for 2-24 hours.

In a large frying pan with a little oil, sauté the onions, mushrooms and garlic until tender, then place into a bowl and chill in the refrigerator.

In a large frying pan with a little oil sauté the rabbit until lightly browned, then place into a bowl and chill in the refrigerator.

Preheat the oven to 250°F (120°C).

Mince the marinated pork through a medium plate mincer and then place 1/4 of the mince into a food processor. Start pureeing the meat while adding the cream to get a smooth farce.

Place the minced pork, onions, extra diced pork, rabbit and onion mix into a large bowl and mix well with your hand until combined.

Place the mix in a ovenproof terrine mould and cover with a lid. Place the terrine mould into a large, high-sided tray and half fill with hot water.

Place into the oven and cook for 2.5-3 hours or until the internal temperature reaches 160°F (72°C).

Once cooked, allow to cool on the bench for 2 hours, then chill for 6 hours or overnight.

Once chilled remove from the terrine mould and slice into ¾ inch (½ cm) slices and serve.

To store, keep in the refrigerator and wrap well with plastic wrap. Use within 6-7 days.

# »ROTISSERIE VENISON RACK

Venison is a lean meat so overcooking it is not recommended. Be careful to keep an eye on the internal temperature and remember things keep cooking a little after you remove them from a heat source. Basting the meat will help with the flavor. To help prevent it becoming too dry you could lard it with pork fat or wrap it in belly bacon (a technique called "barding").

## INGREDIENTS

2 venison racks,
  french-trimmed 4 rib racks
4–5 sprigs thyme
7 oz (200 ml) salt water glaze
  (page 194) in a plastic squirty
  bottle
6–8 juniper berries, crushed
salt and fresh-cracked pepper

**Serves 5–6**

## METHOD

Preheat the rotisserie to 325-350°F (170-180°C).

Season the rack with salt, pepper and juniper berries. Place the thyme sprigs on the rack and with butcher's string tie the rack so that the loin becomes uniform in thickness, this will help with it cooking evenly.

Skew the loin with the rotisserie spit rod and place the rotisserie forks on each end to secure the rack.

Place onto the barbecue rotisserie and cook until at an internal temperature of 125-135°F (52-58°C). While cooking, lightly coat the venison with the salt water glaze every 7-10 minutes. How long it takes to cook the venison will vary depending on the size and thickness of the venison, but it will be usually around the 30-40 minute mark.

Once cooked, remove from the rotisserie and leave to rest for 5-8 minutes.

Carve into cutlets by cutting between the bones.

Serve hot.

# » BARBECUE VENISON HAUNCH

This can be an excellent way to cook for many, simply. Barding, or laying fat over the meat while cooking will help keep the venison moist because it's such a lean meat.

## INGREDIENTS

1 venison haunch, tunnel boned
  4 ½ pounds (2kg)
5 oz (150 g) pork back fat or
  streaky bacon
5 garlic cloves, sliced
  lengthways in half
4–5 sprigs fresh thyme
canola oil, for cooking
salt and freshly-ground black
  pepper

Serves 6–8

## METHOD

Preheat a barbecue with a lid to 325°F (170°C).

Using a small knife insert it into the meat about ¾ inch (2 cm) deep, then insert a piece of garlic, repeat in various parts of the meat until all the garlic is used up.

Lightly coat the venison in oil, then season well with salt and pepper.

Lay the thyme and back fat or bacon over the top, then, using butchers string, tie the fat onto the venison. This will secure the fat and produce a balanced shape to help the meat cook evenly.

Place the venison on wire cake rack and place the rack onto a tray in the barbecue . Place the tray into the barbecue and close the lid.

Keep the temperature steady and cook for 55-65 minutes or until the internal temperature reaches 130°F (55°C). If you like your meat a little more cooked than rare/medium rare, cook until 140°F (60°C).

Let stand for 15-20 minutes, then carve to serve.

# » VENISON SHORT LOIN WITH CRANBERRY COMPOTE

Venison is a meat that lends itself to some sweetness once cooked. Serving venison with a fruit-based compote or sauce really does wonders with it. I often serve it with cranberries, though braised red cabbage and apple also works very well.

## INGREDIENTS

1 loin on venison 2 ¼ pounds (1 kg)
salt and freshly milled pepper
canola oil, for cooking

### Compote

7 oz (200 g) cranberries, frozen
4½ oz (125 g) caster sugar
2¾ oz (80 ml) orange juice
2 cloves
2 sprigs fresh thyme

### Marinade

3½ oz (100 ml) red wine
2 garlic cloves, crushed
3 sprigs fresh thyme
8 peppercorns, crushed
1 bay leaf, roughly chopped

Serves 4–5

## METHOD

In a medium-sized pot bring all the compote ingredients—except the cranberries—to a boil and simmer for 2 minutes. Then add the cranberries and cook for a further 5 minutes on a medium heat.

Allow to cool before serving.

In a plastic ziplock bag add all the ingredients for the marinade with the venison short loin. Remove as much air as possible and marinate in the refrigerator for 4-24 hours.

Preheat the barbecue grill to a medium high heat.

Remove the venison from the marinade and pat dry with paper towel. Lightly oil the venison and season it well with salt and pepper, then grill it on the barbecue for 6-7 minutes each side or until the internal temperature reaches 125-130°F (52-55°C).

Allow to rest for 5-8 minutes and slice into medallions about ¾ inch (2cm) thick.

Serve with the cranberry compote.

# POULTRY

# »LEMON & THYME COATED CHICKEN DRUMS (PF)

Drumsticks are great to take with you to picnics or when invited to family or friends. Excellent served cold so it's no problem if you cook more than you need.

## INGREDIENTS
12–14 chicken drumsticks
canola oil, for cooking

3 oz (80 g) all purpose flour
3 oz (80 g) japanese bread
  crumbs
1 teaspoon salt
1 teaspoon freshly ground black
  pepper
1 teaspoon dried thyme
2 teaspoons lemon zest
½ teaspoon allspice
½ teaspoon smoked paprika
½ teaspoon garlic powder

Serves 4–6

## METHOD
Preheat the barbecue flat plate to a medium heat.

In a large plastic bag, add all the dry ingredients and shake well.

Place the chicken in the bag and shake to coat the chicken drums.

Oil the flat plate and add the chicken to the grill in a single layer.

Turn the chicken every couple of minutes, adding more oil if necessary, until the drumsticks become golden brown.

Cook for 25-35 minutes or until the internal temperature reaches 160°F (72°C)

Serve hot with a simple salad and tomato chutney (page 185).

# »SPLIT CHICKEN WITH ROAST APRICOTS

Fresh apricots and chicken is a good combination—the grilled flavor of the chicken marries well with the sweetness of the apricot. You can make this dish leaving out the brining process but it tends not to be as moist as when you don't brine.

## INGREDIENTS
1 whole chicken, size 20 (2 ¼ pound or 1 kg)
2 quart (2 liters) chicken brine (page 198)
salt and freshly-ground black pepper
canola oil, for cooking
Toasted almonds, for garnish

### Sauce
6 fresh apricots, halved with stones removed
canola oil, for cooking
1 vanilla pod, split
4–6 cardamom pods, cracked
2–3 sprigs fresh thyme
3 tablespoons liquid honey
1 tablespoon lemon juice
4 tablespoons orange juice
3 fl oz (100 ml) water

**Serves 4**

## METHOD

To make the sauce, place all the ingredients except the apricots into a medium-sized pot and bring to a boil. Set aside to cool.

Lightly oil the apricots, then over a medium-high heat, cook or grill the apricot halves for 1-2 minutes on each side, then add them into the sauce mixture.

Using a large knife cut the backbone out of the chicken, then, using a brine pump, inject the brine evenly into the meat and allow it to soak in the brine for 1-24 hours.

Preheat the barbecue to a medium heat.

After soaking, pat the chicken dry, lightly oil and season well with salt and pepper.

Place onto the barbecue bone side down for 30 minutes, then turn on to the skin side for 15-20 minutes or until the internal temperature reaches 160°F (72°C).

Allow to stand for 10 minutes, then cut into pieces and pour over the hot apricot sauce.

Garnish with toasted almonds to serve.

# »HERB-RUBBED ROTISSERIE CHICKEN

Rotisserie chicken is a true classic. I have worked in a few places where this was a staple on the menu and this is one meal I like to make at home because the whole family enjoys it. It's great served with a simple slaw or crispy broccoli salad (page 144).

## INGREDIENTS

1 whole chicken size 20
3 quart (3 liters) chicken brine
6–8 tablespoons chicken rub
2¼ oz (60g) butter

**Serves 4**

## METHOD

Using a meat injector or brine pump, pump the chicken evenly with brine. Then leave it to marinate in the remaining brine for 24 hours.

The following day, pat the chicken dry with paper towels. Truss the chicken up so that the legs are tied together and the winglets are folded under the back of the bird. This helps with even cooking as it stops the legs flaying about and cooking too quickly before the rest of the bird is ready.

Using your fingers, free the skin from the breasts then put some rub between the skin and the breasts. Place half the butter under the skin on each side.

Coat the rest of the chicken with an even layer of the chicken rub.

Allow to stand for 20-30 minutes before cooking.

Preheat a barbecue with a rotisserie attachment to 325-350°F (170-180°C).

Place the chicken onto the spit rod shaft and securely clamp it between the spit forks. If the chicken is not secured tightly to the shaft the chicken will fail to turn correctly and not cook evenly.

Place the chicken onto the rotisserie and allow it to cook over indirect heat for 1-1.5 hours or until it has an internal temperature of 160°F (72°C).

Remove from the rotisserie and let it stand for 5-10 minutes before serving.

# »SPICED SPLIT CHICKEN BREASTS

These are an excellent addition to any burger or grilled sandwich. They cook quite quickly and taste great. The key is not to overcook them as chicken breast is lean and will become dry if overcooked. This recipe makes an excellent little tapas dish if hte breast is cut into strips and served with aioli (see page 181).

## INGREDIENTS
4 large chicken breasts, skin off
1 quart (1 liter) chicken brine
6 tablespoons chicken rub (see
   page 198)
canola oil, for cooking

**Serves 4**

## METHOD
Slice the chicken breasts lengthways into two flat pieces and wrap each piece between two sheets of plastic wrap. Once wrapped, gently flatten the pieces a little using the back of a saucepan, meat tenderizer or rolling pin.

Place the chicken pieces into the brine for 2-24 hours.

Remove from the brine and pat dry with paper towels.

Preheat a barbecue flat plate to a medium-high heat.

Liberally coat the chicken pieces in the rub and let them stand for 15 minutes before cooking.

Oil the plate and place the chicken breasts in a single layer.

Allow to cook for 3-4 minutes on each side or until the meat has cooked through remember, not too much.

Rest for 2-3 minutes before serving.

# »BARBECUED BUFFALO WINGS

A real American classic, usually deep fried but just as good cooked on the barbecue, these can be a little too spicy for some people! If you wish to tone down the heat go easy on the cayenne.

## INGREDIENTS
16 whole chicken wings

### Marinade
5 oz (150 g) barbecue sauce
  (see page 184)
1 teaspoon cayenne pepper
1 tablespoon smoked paprika
¼ teaspoon freshly-ground black
  pepper
½ teaspoon salt
3 tablespoons canola oil

Serves 4–6

## METHOD
In a large bowl mix all the marinade ingredients together.

Prepare the chicken by cutting off the winglets ( the very tips of the wings -discard these or save them for stock).

Cut each wing through the joint and marinate them for 30–40 minutes at room temperature.

Heat the barbecue to a medium heat, place the chicken into a deep-sided tray and place the tray into the barbecue on an indirect heat. Cook for around 25 minutes or until the juices run clear, turning every 5 minutes.

Once cooked, serve with extra barbecue sauce for dipping.

# »WHOLE BARBECUE DUCK WITH ORANGE

Duck with orange is a classic combination of flavors. The glaze gives the skin a lovely color and flavor and also helps with the crispiness. A great way to enjoy duck!

## INGREDIENTS
1 large whole duck
2 oranges, quartered
4 sprigs thyme
2 whole star anise
salt for seasoning

### Glaze
2 tablespoons orange juice
1 tablespoon liquid honey
1 tablespoon cider vinegar

**SERVES 3–4**

## METHOD
Mix together all the ingredients for the duck in a small bowl and set aside.

Pat the duck dry with paper towels, then stuff the orange, thyme and star anise into the duck cavity.

Season with salt and let rest for an hour.

Preheat the barbecue to 300°F (150°C).

Place the duck onto a tray and slowly cook on the barbecue on an indirect heat for 1 hour.

To make the glaze, combine the glaze ingredients and mix in a bowl until well combined.

After cooking for an hour, keep duck on barbecue and brush with the glaze every 10 minutes of cooking, until the breast reaches an internal temperature of 160°F (72°C).

Remove from the barbecue and rest for 5 minutes before carving.

# »SPICY BARBECUE DUCK

This is a delicious duck recipe and it will help if you have a thermometer to get the right finishing temperature. If you want to have it without the chili just remove it from the spice mix. Like all recipes, feel free to change and modify to your taste.

## INGREDIENTS
1 large whole duck

### Glaze
2 tablespoons liquid honey
1 tablespoon soy sauce
1 tablespoon hoisin sauce

### Spice mix
1 teaspoon salt
1 teaspoon five spice
1 teaspoon chili flakes
1 teaspoon freshly-ground black pepper

**Serves 3–4**

## METHOD

To make the glaze, mix all the ingredients together in a small bowl and set aside.

Mix all the spices together in a another small bowl and set aside.

Remove the duck from its packaging and pat dry with paper towels. Place onto a plate then brush generously with the glaze and leave uncovered in the refrigerator for at least 2 hours to allow the duck to dry. Leave overnight if possible for a better result.

Preheat the barbecue to 300-320°F (150-160°C).

Rub the spice mix onto the duck and place onto a tray and then put the duck into the barbecue on an indirect heat and cover with the lid. Cook until the internal temperature of the breast is at 155°F (70°C); this should take around 1 hour 20 minutes.

Remove from the barbecue and let stand for 5 minutes before carving.

# »BARBECUED SPLIT QUAIL WITH GARLIC CHIVE DRESSING

Quails are very tasty and this way of cooking them is a little faster than roasting them whole. It's also a great dish to serve as a shared meal, or a pot-luck dinner, and is very easy to do.

## INGREDIENTS
8–10 large quails
canola oil, for cooking
salt and freshly-ground black
   pepper

### Dressing
6 tablespoons extra-virgin olive
   oil
2 tablespoons lemon juice
2 garlic cloves, crushed
1 small bunch chives, chopped
salt and freshly-ground black
   pepper

**Serves 4**

## METHOD
First spilt the quails by placing back side down. Use a medium size knife to go lengthwise through the middle of the quail and slice through the back, then turn over and slice through the breast.

Heat the barbecue to a medium heat.

Lightly oil the quails on all sides and season well with salt and pepper to taste.

Place them on the grill, skin side down, and cook for 4-5 minutes, then turn over and cook for another 12-15 minutes with the lid down.

At this stage they should be ready. If you are unsure use a small knife and slice into one of the breasts to test doneness. It should be cooked but still a little pink.

Place all the dressing ingredients into a large bowl and whisk them together. Once the quails are cooked toss them in the dressing and serve warm.

# »ASIAN SPICED DUCK BREAST (PF)

These duck breasts can be eaten hot or cold. Once chilled they can be sliced thinly at an angle and arranged on a plate, so if you end up with too many they can always be used the following day.

## INGREDIENTS
6 large duck breasts
salt, for seasoning

## Spice marinade
4 tablespoons olive oil
1 tablespoon sesame oil
1 tablespoon soy sauce
1 teaspoon crushed ginger
1 garlic clove, crushed
½ teaspoon five spice, ground
1 teaspoon salt
¼ teaspoon freshly ground black pepper

Serves 6

## METHOD
Mix all of the spice marinade ingredients together in a medium-sized bowl and set aside.

Using a sharp knife, score the skins of the duck breasts but be careful to cut the skin and fat only and not to cut into the meat.

Put aside ¼ of the marinade and reserve for brushing the duck breasts when cooking. Marinate the duck breasts in the remaining ¾ of the marinade for at least 2 hours.

Heat a barbecue flat plate to a medium heat.

Season the skin side of the breasts with salt and place them skin side down onto the barbecue. Allow them to grill for 8 minutes, then turn them over and allow them to cook for a further 8 minutes.

Brush wiht marinade and turn again to the skin side for 4 minutes and then follow with one last turn to cook for a further 4 minutes.

To check whether the breasts are cooked enough, make a small slice with a sharp knife halfway on the breast. If the meat is pink then they are done. If not, return to the grill and cook for a few minutes until done to your satisfaction but take care not to overcook.

Brush with the remaining marinade and rest for 5 minutes before serving with Sweet Potato and Créme Fraiche Salad (see page 143).

# »BARBECUE ROAST QUAIL

It's always good to cook a few extra quails as sometimes two is not quite enough. With all the small bones they require a little patience to eat, but it's worth the effort as they taste so good.

## INGREDIENTS
8–10 large quails
canola oil, for cooking
salt and freshly-ground black
  pepper

## Dressing
3 sprigs thyme
3 oz (80g) butter

**Serves 4**

## METHOD

Mix the thyme and butter together in a small bowl, season well and set aside.

Heat the barbecue to 325°F (170–175°C).

In a lightly-oiled, ovenproof tray place all the quails and lightly coat them with oil. Season well and top with extra thyme sprigs, then place them into the barbecue and cover with the lid. Cook for 25-30 minutes or until the juices run a pale pink when you insert a skewer into the leg.

Once done, add the butter and thyme to the tray and allow it to melt, then baste the quails for a minute or so with the melted butter. You can used smoked butter (page 183) if you'd like to try that variation.

Place onto your serving tray and serve hot.

# »BARBECUED ROAST PHEASANT

When roasting you will need a barbecue that has a cover or lid to keep the heat in and to produce a oven-like environment. This is a great way to cook while the weather is good and allows you to spend some time in the sun while getting your meal ready.

If you are buying the pheasant, get your butcher to tie the bird for you. If you are lucky enough to have caught it yourself, truss the legs to make sure the meat cooks evenly during roasting.

## INGREDIENTS
2 whole pheasants, trussed
8 rashers belly bacon
16 fl oz (500 ml) chicken stock
2¼ oz (60 g) butter or oil for
   canola oil, for cooking
salt and freshly-ground black
   pepper

Serves 4

## METHOD
Preheat the barbecue to 300–320°F (150–160°C)

Lightly rub the birds with a little oil and place them into a large, lightly-oiled roasting pan.

Place half the butter onto the breasts of the birds and then lay over 4 rashers of bacon onto each of the pheasants.

Season with salt and pepper then pour the chicken stock into the pan.

Place the pan into the barbecue for 1.5 hours or until you are able to twist the leg bone and have it come away from the meat.

Once cooked, remove the pheasant from the pan, turn the barbecue on high and allow the stock to reduce until it's the consistency of a slightly thick sauce.

Carve the pheasant as you would a chicken and serve hot with the sauce.

# »JERK CHICKEN WITH MANGO & CHILI SALSA

This is a great barbecue meal. The marinade takes a few ingredients to make but the results are well worth the effort.

## INGREDIENTS
8 large chicken breasts, skin on

**Jerk chicken marinade**
1 teaspoon allspice
1 teaspoon thyme dried
1 teaspoon freshly-ground black pepper
1 teaspoon sage dried
¼ teaspoon cinnamon ground
¼ teaspoon nutmeg ground
½ teaspoon cayenne pepper
1 teaspoon garlic powder
2 teaspoon salt
2 fl oz (60 ml) lime juice
5 fl oz (150 ml) orange juice
2 fl oz (60 ml) soya sauce
8 fl oz (250 ml) olive oil
7 fl oz (200 ml) white wine vinegar
1 large white onion, finely diced
3 garlic cloves, crushed

7 oz (200 g) Mango & Chili Salsa (see page 190)

Serves 6–8

## METHOD
Holding your knife on a 30° angle to the long center line of the breasts, slice each breast into 4-5 pieces.

To make the marinade, combine all of the ingredients in a bowl and mix well.

Place the chicken in the marinade and coat all of them chicken before separating the pieces. Allow to marinate in the refrigerator for at least 3 hours but for up to 24 hours if you have the opportunity.

Preheat the barbecue to a medium high heat. You can use either a flat plate or grill for the cooking.

Remove the chicken from the marinade and place it on the grill in single layer, skin side up, and cook for 3-4 minutes on each side or until the chicken is cooked through.

Place onto a serving plate, serve hot and top with the Mango and Chili Salsa.

# FISH & SHELLFISH

# » GRILLED CLAMS WITH WHITE WINE, GARLIC AND CHILI

As with a lot of seafood, clams are cooked quickly and are best served right away. Great as a starter when having a few friends around and best eaten with a small fork and your fingers. Use a barbecue with a lid to help the clams cook evenly.

## INGREDIENTS
36 large, fresh live clams
3 fl oz (100 ml) white wine

3 garlic cloves, finely sliced
pinch chili flakes
1½ oz (40 g) butter, cut in small cubes
2 tablespoons Italian parsley, coarsely chopped
freshly-ground black pepper

Serves 2–3

## METHOD
Place the clams into cold water for 15-20 minutes to help remove any sand from the shells.

Preheat your flat top barbecue or grill to a high heat, then add the drained clams in a single layer on the barbecue and top with the wine. Close the lid and allow to steam for 3-4 minutes or until they have just opened.

Place the cooked clams into a large bowl and add the remaining ingredients, season lightly and mix well.

Serve hot.

# » SQUID WITH CORN & CHILI SALAD (PF)

Flash-grilled squid is a fast meal. I always have some squid dish on the menu because it only takes seconds to cook and it's always popular – a real crowd pleaser!

## INGREDIENTS
7–8 large squid tubes
2 tablespoons lemon juice
3 tablespoons extra-virgin olive oil
1 tablespoon Italian parsley, coarsely chopped

### Corn and chili salad
6 corn cobs, grilled (page 132)
1 small red onion, finely diced
6 vine-ripened tomatoes, diced
1 small bunch fresh coriander (cilantro), chopped
1 red chili, finely chopped
4 tablespoons olive oil
2 tablespoons red wine vinegar
canola oil, for cooking
salt and freshly-ground black pepper

Serves 5–6

## METHOD

Lay the squid on the chopping board with the ends at the top and bottom.

Place the knife on the inside of the tube and slice from the bottom upwards to open up the tube. Remove any innards that might still be in the tube. Score the squid in a crosshatch pattern with a knife taking care only to cut halfway through the flesh.

Once scored, slice the squid from left to right—this will ensure that the squid stays in long pieces. Squid curls from top to tail.

Heat the flat plate to high, lightly toss the squid in a little oil, then place the pieces evenly on the barbecue and cook for 30-40 seconds, turning once only, then remove from the heat and place into a medium size bowl. Add the lemon and oil and season well.

Serve warm with the salad.

### For the salad
Slice the kernels from the corn cobs and place in a medium bowl. Add the remaining ingredients, seasoning to taste with salt and pepper.

# » GRILLED SALMON FILLETS (PF)

Salmon is a wonderful fish grilled on the barbecue, you can either use a flat plate or grill plate to cook it. This is another item you can take with you for your picnic or outdoor meal.

## INGREDIENTS

4 salmon fillets, skinless, each 6 oz (175 g)
10 fl oz (300 ml) fish brine #2 (see page 199)
2 tablespoons apple syrup
salt and freshly-ground black pepper

**Serves 4**

## METHOD

Place the salmon fillets into the brine for 20-30 minutes to allow them to cure.

Preheat the barbecue to a medium heat.

After brining, remove the salmon and and lightly oil and season with salt and pepper.

Place the salmon skin-side up on the barbecue, grill for 4-5 minutes and then turn over. Brush with the apple syrup and cook for a further 4-5 minutes.

To check that the salmon is done, place the tip of a small knife into the thickest part of the fillet and leave it there for 5 seconds, remove the blade and if the blade is warm then the salmon is medium rare; if the blade is hot then it's well done. I like to cook the salmon medium rare to medium. Doing it this way will allow you to adjust the cooking to your liking because you can't uncook a fish!

Best served hot with some crusty bread and salad.

# » TUNA STEAKS WITH BEAN & RED ONION SALSA

Tuna is a great fish for the barbecue. It's best served very rare as any further cooking tends to make it dry. The aioli is a nice touch and acts like a sauce for this dish.

## INGREDIENTS

4 tuna steaks 8 oz (225 g),
  1–1½ inches (3–4 cm) thick
14 oz (400 g) green beans,
  trimmed and blanched
1 large red onion, rinsed with
  cold water then thinly sliced
½ oz (15 g) Italian parsley,
  coarsely chopped
20 black olives, stone removed
2 teaspoon capers
3 tablespoons red wine vinegar
3 tablespoons extra-virgin olive
  oil
canola oil, for cooking
salt and freshly-ground black
  pepper
4 tablespoons aioli (page 181)

**SERVES 4**

## METHOD

In a large bowl mix the beans, red onion, parsley, olives, capers, vinegar and extra-virgin olive oil and season well.

Preheat the barbecue or grill to high.

Lightly coat the tuna with oil and season well. Be liberal with the salt and pepper.

Place the tuna steak onto the grill and leave for 3 minutes then turn over and cook a further 3 minutes.

Now sear on the sides for about 10–15 seconds on each side until the steak is lightly browned all over.

Leave to rest for 2–3 minutes.

While resting, divide the salad onto four plates.

Top with the tuna and aioli.

Serve warm.

# »SCALLOPS WITH LEMON & CHIVE BUTTER

I really enjoy scallop season. Nothing beats freshly shucked scallops cooked simply. Just a little chive butter is all that they really need. Try these with the Grilled Fennel and Red Onion Salad (page 148).

## INGREDIENTS
24 scallops, freshly shucked
canola oil for cooking
salt

## Lemon Chive Butter
2¼ oz (60 g) butter, softened
1 lemon juiced
½ oz (15 g) chives, finely
  chopped
salt and freshly-ground black
  pepper

**Serves 4**

## METHOD
In a medium-sized bowl mix the butter, lemon juice and chives together and season well then set aside.

Place the scallops onto a paper towel and pat dry. Having them dry will help them brown up more when grilling.

Preheat a flat plate barbecue to medium heat. Lightly oil the plate and evenly place the scallops on the hot surface. Season with salt and allow to cook for 1 minute, then turn. After 30 seconds add the chive butter to the scallops.

After 30 seconds remove the scallops and serve hot.

# » WHOLE GRILLED SNAPPER

Grilling whole is a great way to cook fish. It helps keep the flesh moist and the end result makes for an impressive centerpiece to any barbecue. It also allows people to take off only the amount they wish to eat and lets those who enjoy eating the special bits like the "cheeks" to have their choice as well.

## INGREDIENTS

1 whole snapper 5½ lb (2.5 kg), gilled, gutted and scaled
2 lemons, sliced into 5 round slices each
2 red chilies, sliced into 5 long pieces each
1 small bunch coriander (cilantro)
1 small bunch Italian parsley
salt and freshly-ground black pepper
canola oil for cooking
8 inch (20 cm) wooden skewer

## Butter Sauce

5 oz (150 g) butter
1 lemon, juiced
2 tablespoons coriander (cilantro), coarsely chopped
2 tablespoons Italian parsley, coarsely chopped

**Serves 6–8**

## METHOD

Preheat the barbecue grill to a medium heat. If you have a barbecue with a lid it will help cook the snapper a little faster.

To make the sauce, place the butter and lemon juice into a small pot over the barbecue, ensuring that the handle is away from the heat. Once the butter starts to boil, remove from the heat and add the herbs. Set aside and keep warm.

Score the snapper on both sides by slicing through skin—though not quite through to the backbone—about 3-4 times on each side.

Stuff the lemons, chili, coriander and parsley into the stomach cavity. Use the skewer to truss the belly shut.

Lightly oil both sides of the fish and place it onto the grill. Turn the grill to a low heat and cook for 13-–15 minutes on each side or until the flesh has turned white. You can check this by using a small knife to pierce the fish, then move the knife while in the flesh to one side to check the color close to the backbone.

Place the fish onto a serving dish and pour over the butter sauce to serve.

# »MUSSELS WITH GARLIC & HERB DRESSING (PF)

Mussels are great for taking on picnics and this is another dish that can be prepared quickly when time is short. The mussels can be cooked the day prior and stored in the refrigerator ready for use. Using a barbecue with a lid will help the mussels cook evenly and faster.

## INGREDIENTS

36 fresh green-lipped mussels, scrubbed and de-bearded
3 fl oz (100 ml) white wine

### Marinade

7 oz (200 g) palm sugar
7 oz (200 ml) white wine vinegar
½ oz (15 g) fresh ginger, peeled and finely sliced
3 garlic cloves, finely sliced
1 red chili, finely sliced with seeds
2 limes, zest and juice
1 small bunch coriander (cilantro), coarsely chopped

**Serves 4 as an entrée – 2 as a main**

## METHOD

Using a medium-sized pot over a high heat, bring the sugar and vinegar to a boil, then add the ginger, garlic, chili and lime and simmer for 1 minute, before removing the pot from heat and allow to cool to room temperature. Once cool, add in the coriander.

Preheat a barbecue flat plate to a high heat.

Place the mussels in a single layer on the barbecue and pour over the white wine. Then close the lid of the barbecue for 2–3 minutes or until the mussels have opened. Remove the mussels and place them into a large bowl and allow them to cool for a few minutes.

Remove the mussel meat from the shells and place into the prepared marinade. Chill for 1 hour before eating. They marinated mussels can be kept for 2–3 days in the refrigerator.

# » GRILLED CRAYFISH WITH SMOKED PAPRIKA BUTTER

Crayfish is a real treat and I believe that the best way to cook it is very simply. Baking crayfish with herb butter is a classic and this is my twist on this recipe. Using a barbecue with a lid will be helpful but it's not essential to the success of this dish.

## INGREDIENTS

1 crayfish 3¼ lb (1.4 kg), raw and green
2¼ oz (60 g) smoked butter (page 183)
1 teaspoon smoked paprika
1 lemon
salt and freshly-ground black pepper
canola oil, for cooking

Serves 2

## METHOD

Preheat the barbecue or grill to a high heat.

To prepare, cut the crayfish with a large knife or cleaver lengthways, through its head first and then tail. Remove the tomalley (innards) from the interior of the body of the crayfish.

Drizzle the flesh sides of the crayfish with a little canola oil and place this side down on a hot grill for 2–3 minutes to color well. Then turn the crayfish over and into the two halves, in the cavity left from where you have removed the tomalley, place the butter evenly and then dust the butter with paprika. Squeeze the juice of half a lemon onto each side. Season well and then cook for a further 5–7 minutes or until the flesh in the center of the tail has turned from opaque to white.

Once cooked, serve hot.

# »GROUPER STEAKS WITH HERB CRUST

I first saw this dish 20 years ago and still believe that it's a great way of eating grouper. It's very simple and the herbs really complement the meaty texture of fish.

## INGREDIENTS
4 x grouper (Hapuka) 8 oz (220 g) steaks, 1–1.5 in (3–4 cm)
canola oil for cooking
1½ oz (40 g) butter

### Herb crust
½ teaspoon dried thyme
½ teaspoon dried sage
½ teaspoon dried oregano
½ teaspoon dried kelp salt
½ teaspoon dried paprika
2 tablespoons dried bread crumbs
¼ teaspoon cayenne pepper

**Serves 4**

## METHOD
For the herb crust mix all the ingredients together.

Preheat a barbecue flat plate to medium, then lightly oil it. Then take each grouper steak and press the non-skin side down into the herb mix, coating the surface well.

Place the seasoned grouper onto the hot plate. Repeat for all the steaks.

Cook for 3-4 minutes on one side then turn over. Top the herb crust with a knob of butter and leave to cook for another 3-4 minutes.

If your barbecue has a lid, place this down after you turn the fish to help cook it through. Aim for an internal temperature of around 140°F (60°C).

Serve hot.

# » ASIAN-STYLE GRILLED GARFISH (PIPER) (PF)

This is another simple fish dish which does not take a lot of time to prepare. You can ask your fish supplier to gut and clean and scale the fish and they may even score it for you if you ask nicely! This is a great dish to bring to any barbecue or picnic. Allowing the garfish to marinate for a time in the sauce will improve the flavor even more.

## INGREDIENTS

4 small garfish, gutted, cleaned and scaled
salt and freshly-ground black pepper
canola oil, for cooking

### Sauce

3 fl oz (100 ml) olive oil
3 tablespoons honey
1 small red onion finely sliced
2 chilies, seeds removed and finely sliced
3 limes, zest and juice
1 tablespoon ginger, freshly grated
2 teaspoon fish sauce
2 tablespoons coriander coarsely chopped
2 teaspoon sesame oil
freshly-ground black pepper

**Serves 4 as an appetiser – 2 as a main**

## METHOD

Whisk together all the sauce ingredients. If you like your dishes on the sweet side add more honey. If you like a bit more tang then add another lime. Season with pepper and set aside.

Heat the barbecue to a medium-high heat.

Score the fish on each side around 3-4 times but not so deep as to reach the bones.

Brush the fish with a little oil and lightly season with salt and pepper.

Grill the fish for around 5-6 minutes on each side until lightly charred and the flesh easily comes away from the bones.

Once cooked, place on a serving plate and dress with the sauce, allow to stand a few minutes before serving.

# VEGETABLES & SALADS

# » GRILLED CORNCOBS WITH SMOKED BUTTER

Grilled corn is a real delight! Cooked in the husks helps prevent it from drying out and the smoked butter gives it a beautiful taste. Season well because corn needs the salt.

## INGREDIENTS
6 corncobs in husks
5 oz (150 g) smoked butter
  (page 183), softened

**Serves 6**

## METHOD
Carefully peel back the corn husks, keeping them attached to the cob, be sure to remove all the silky strands underneath.

To stop the corn from drying out and to help with the seasoning, pour enough water into a large bowl to soak the corn. Add 1 tablespoon of salt to every liter of water used. Stir until the salt has dissolved, then soak the corncobs, with husks attached for 1 hour.

Pat the corn cobs dry and lightly brush the corn with oil and season with salt and pepper.

Gently pull the husks back over the cobs.

Place on the corncobs on a grill, over a medium-high heat and grill for 15–20 minutes, turning every 3–4 minutes or until the corn is tender. Use a small knife to pierce the corn kernels to check this at the 15 minute mark.

Once the corn is tender, remove the husks and liberally brush with the smoked butter. Lightly season and serve hot.

# » GRILLED VEGETABLE SALAD (PF)

This is one of my favorite salads. It's quick and easy to prepare with great results. It matches any barbecue meats and is always well received at picnics or parties.

## INGREDIENTS

2 aubergines (eggplant) cut into
  ½-inch (1 cm) discs
2 red capsicums deseeded,
  and cut into 8–10 small,
  rectangular-shaped pieces
2 red onions, peeled, cut in
  wedges, keeping the core
4 zucchinis (courgettes) cut
  into ½-inch (1 cm) slices on
  the angle
10–15 fresh, large basil leaves
½ oz (15 g) fresh Italian parsley,
  roughly chopped
3–4 tablespoons olive oil
3 tablespoons balsamic vinegar
salt and freshly-ground black
  pepper
canola oil for cooking

Serves 6

## METHOD

Heat the barbecue to a medium-high heat and lightly oil the vegetables, then grill until tender.

Cut the eggplant discs into halves and place all the vegetables into a large bowl.

Add the herbs and dress with the oil and balsamic vinegar mixture and season well.

Gently toss together.

Serve warm.

# » MUSHROOMS, GARLIC & BALSAMIC SALAD

This salad is easy to make while you are cooking your meats or whenever you have a spare few minutes. It's a simple, tasty salad and it's best served warm—great with any steak or chop that you're cooking on the barbecue.

## INGREDIENTS
12 flat mushrooms, medium sized, brushed to remove soil

### Dressing
3 garlic cloves, crushed
½ oz (10 g) parsley, roughly chopped
½ oz (10 g) fresh chives
3½ fl oz (100 ml) balsamic vinegar
3½ oz (100 ml) olive oil
salt and freshly-ground black pepper
canola oil for cooking

Serves 4–6

## METHOD
To make the dressing, mix the garlic, herbs, balsamic vinegar and olive oil together in a small bowl.

Heat the barbecue to a medium heat. Lightly brush the mushrooms with oil and grill top side down for 1-2 minutes. Brush the mushrooms with the dressing then turn over and cook for a further 2 minutes.

Turn again every minute until the mushrooms are softened. During this time brush the mushrooms again with the dressing everytime you turn them over.

Place the mushrooms on a serving dish and pour over the remaining dressing. Season well and let stand for 5 minutes before serving.

# » BARBECUED ASPARAGUS SALAD WITH CURED BACON & SOFT-BOILED EGGS

Asparagus season is short so it's best to make the most of it when it arrives. This is a simple way of serving it and it is very tasty. It can easily be done on a grill pan for similar results to barbecuing if the weather's not conducive to lighting up the barbecue.

## INGREDIENTS

17½ oz (500 g) asparagus, trimmed
8 slices dry-cured and smoked belly bacon
4 eggs
½ oz (10 g) chives finely sliced
3 oz (75 g) butter, melted
canola oil for cooking
salt and freshly-ground black pepper

Serves 4

## METHOD

Heat a medium pot of water on the stove and bring it to a boil. Add the eggs, turn down the heat to medium and cook the eggs for 5-6 minutes.

Remove the eggs from the pot and cool under running cold water for 5 minutes (this will help stop the eggs from sticking to the shell), then peel.

Heat the grill plate on the barbecue to medium-high heat.

Place the asparagus in a large bowl and lightly oil, then grill the asparagus until tender, turning every minute or so.

The asparagus should only take 3-4 minutes to cook to the point where it's lightly charred and tender.

Place the asparagus and bacon on your serving plate. Cut the eggs in half and place with the asparagus and top with bacon. Mix the chives and butter together and use it to dress the asparagus.

Season lightly and serve warm.

# »GRILLED CARROT & FETA SALAD (PF)

This is a salad I have enjoyed meals at Ima Cuisine – one of my favorite places to eat in Auckland, New Zealand. Yael, the owner, takes great pride in what she makes and in my opinion, this is one of her best dishes.

## INGREDIENTS

8 large carrots, topped, tailed, peeled and halved, then sliced into 2-inch (5 cm) strips ways for a total net weight of about 2¼ pounds (1 kg)
3½ oz (100 g) feta, diced
4½ oz (125 g) black olives
¾ oz (20 g) Italian parsley roughly chopped
4 tablespoons lemon juice
4 tablespoons extra-virgin olive oil
canola oil, for cooking

**Serves 6–8**

## METHOD

Preheat the barbecue grill to a medium heat.

In a large bowl toss the carrots with some canola oil to lightly coat them and then season well with salt and pepper.

Grill the carrots for about 25-30 minutes or until the carrots are tender and still have a little crunch.

Slice the carrots pieces and place in a large bowl. Dress with the olive oil and lemon juice.

Gently mix in the feta and olives and season if necessary.

This salad can be served warm or room temperature.

# »SWEET POTATO & CRÈME FRAICHE SALAD (PF)

This recipe has always received compliments, people comment on how tasty it is, and how easy it is to make. It pairs well with salmon, pork and lamb.

## INGREDIENTS
2 large sweet potatoes (kumara) with a total net weight of about 1 ¾ lb (800 g), peeled and diced into small cubes
1½ fl oz (40 ml) olive oil
4½ oz (125 g) crème fraiche – if crème fraiche isn't available you can try yogurt or sour cream or a half-and-half blend of the two
12 cherry tomatoes (halved)
3½ oz (100 g) red onion finely sliced
1 spring onion, finely sliced
salt and freshly-ground black pepper

**Serves 4–6**

## METHOD
Heat the flat grill plate of a barbecue to a low heat.

In a large container add the sweet potatoe and lightly oil.

Place the sweet potato on the grill and grill for about 8-10 minutes or until tender, continually turning it to color all the sides.

Once cooked, place the sweet potato into a large bowl and season well. Add the crème fraiche, cherry tomatoes, red onion and spring onion.

Mix gently together and season if necessary.

Serve warm.

# » CRISPY BROCCOLI WITH GARLIC & CAPER SALAD

This salad is very quick and really tasty. I like to grow broccoli and this is the most common way it is cooked at my house. My partner, Natalie, made this for me once and now it's become a staple dish.

## INGREDIENTS

2 heads of broccoli sliced into bite-sized pieces with the stem still attached
3 garlic cloves, sliced
2 tablespoons capers
2 tablespoons olive oil
2 tablespoons lemon juice
3–4 tablespoons canola oil
salt and pepper

**Serves 4**

## METHOD

Preheat a barbecue flat plate to a medium-high heat. You can also use a thick-bottomed frying pan.

Add the oil and then the broccoli. Fry for 2 minutes, stirring every 30 seconds or so, then add the garlic and capers and cook for another 1-2 minutes or until the broccoli is lightly charred and tender but not soft.

Dress with the olive oil and lemon.

Place onto your serving dish.

Best served hot.

# »BARBECUED SMOKY PUMPKIN SALAD (PF)

This is my take on a roast pumpkin salad. With the barbecue you can achieve a better color on the pumpkin and the addition of smoke improves the final result.

## INGREDIENTS
½ crown pumpkin (or any of the large, grey-skinned pumpkins), peeled, deseeded and cut into 1–1½ inch (2–3 cm) cubes for a total weight of around 2 lb (1 kg)
4½ oz (125 g) red onion, finely sliced
3½ oz (100 g) feta, crumbled
½ oz (10 gm) Italian parsley, coarsely chopped
3 tablespoons red wine vinegar
4 tablespoons extra-virgin olive oil
canola oil for cooking
salt and freshly-ground black pepper

Serves 6–8

## METHOD
Heat the flat grill plate of a barbecue to a low heat.

In a large bowl, lightly coat the pumpkin with some oil, salt and pepper.

Grill the pumpkin for about 8-10 minutes or until tender, continually turning to color all the sides.

For a smoky flavor, finish the cooking process with a handful of wood chips on the fire and a closed lid for the last minute or so.

In another large bowl mix the red wine vinegar and extra-virgin olive oil together then add the pumpkin, feta and parsley.

Gently toss together and season well.

Serve warm.

# » GRILLED FENNEL & PICKLED RED ONION SALAD (PF)

This fresh, sweet and savory salad works well with grilled fish. I have often used it with grilled snapper and served it as a base instead of a heavy starch (like mashed potato) to make a light meal for warm, summer evenings.

## INGREDIENTS

4 bulbs fennel, finely sliced with core attached with a total weight of around 1½ lb (700 g)

7 oz (200 g) pickled red onion (page 188)

4 tablespoons Italian parsley, coarsely chopped

3 tablespoons lemon juice

4 tablespoons extra-virgin olive oil

canola oil, for cooking

salt and freshly-ground black pepper

**Serves 4–6**

## METHOD

Preheat a flatplate to a high heat. You can also use a thick bottom frying pan for this recipe.

Lightly coat the fennel with oil then grill for 1-2 minutes on the barbecue, the fennel should still be firm to the bite with a little wilting

Toss all the ingredients together, season well and serve warm.

# » CHARRED BRUSSELS SPROUTS SALAD

When Brussels sprouts are charred they taste wonderful—even people who say they don't like them can be tempted. I think this is one of the best ways to serve them.

## INGREDIENTS

1 ⅓ lb (600 g) Brussels sprouts, cut in half lengthways
4 rashers of belly bacon cut into ½ inch (1 cm) pieces
3 garlic cloves, crushed
4 tablespoons balsamic vinegar
4 tablespoons extra-virgin olive oil
canola oil, for cooking
salt and freshly-ground black pepper

**Serves 4–6**

## METHOD

Preheat a barbecue flatplate to a medium heat. You can also use a thick-bottomed frying pan for this recipe.

Lightly oil the flat plate and fry the bacon for 2–3 minutes, then transfer the rashers into a large bowl.

Re-oil the flat plate and add the Brussels sprouts on it, keeping them to a single layer if possible.

Cook the sprouts until golden brown, tender and a little charred. If you find the sprouts are getting too dark without becoming tender then turn down the heat.

Once they are a little charred and tender add in the garlic and balsamic vinegar and cook for 1 minute. Remove from the flat plate and add to the bacon. Season well and add the extra-virgin olive oil.

Gently toss together and serve warm.

# » GRILLED COURGETTE & OLIVE SALAD

This warm salad is a great way to use courgettes (zucchinis) when in season. It's a quick and easy dish for when you want to spend less time cooking and more time enjoying the company of your guests.

## INGREDIENTS

6 courgettes (zucchinis), topped and tailed, sliced on the angle ½ inch (1 cm) thick for a total weight of around 1½ lb (700 g)

5 oz (150 g) kalamata olives

4½ oz (125 g) red onion, finely sliced

½ oz (10 g) Italian parsley coarsely chopped

¼ oz (5 g) fresh mint, coarsely chopped

2 tablespoons lemon juice

3 tablespoons extra-virgin olive oil

canola oil, for cooking

Serves 4–6

## METHOD

Preheat a griddle plate to a medium high heat. You can also use a thick-bottomed griddle pan.

In a large bowl toss the courgettes with a little canola oil to lightly coat them and then season with salt and pepper.

Grill the courgettes on the barbecue for around 1-2 minutes on each side or until tender then set aside.

Place all the remaining ingredients into a large bowl and gently mix together. Lastly, toss in the courgettes, dress with a mixture of the lemon juice and extra-virgin olive oil and serve warm.

# SWEET THINGS

# »BAKED APPLES WITH DRIED FRUIT & BROWN SUGAR

These are a great winter treat, very easy to make and best served with a fresh vanilla sauce or ice cream. By incorporating some rolled oats into the fruit mixture they can be served for brunch.

## INGREDIENTS
4 Granny Smith apples
1 oz (25 g) raisins
1 oz (25 g) dates chopped
1 oz (25 g) diced apricots
¼ teaspoon cinnamon, ground
¼ teaspoon allspice, ground
2 oz (50 g) walnut pieces
2 oz (50 g) brown sugar
pinch of nutmeg, ground
1½ oz (40 g) butter

Serves 4

## METHOD
Preheat barbecue with a lid or your oven to 325°F (170°C).

Line a shallow ovenproof tray with baking paper. Core the apples and place them in the tray.

Mix the dried fruit, spices and sugar together and stuff in the cored apples. Top with a little butter on each apple.

Place 8 fl oz (250 ml) of water in the bottom of the tray and bake for 20-30 minutes or until the apples are soft.

Serve hot to warm with vanilla sauce or ice cream.

# »BAKED BANANA & ICE CREAM

I used to make this dessert years ago while working my apprenticeship. It is a great way to use up those bananas that are starting to go lightly brown (because after they're cooked no one will know that they were a little overripe). The secret is cooking them in their skins!

## INGREDIENTS
4 ripe bananas
4 large scoops of your favorite ice cream
4 tablespoons toasted almonds

## Optional variations
chocolate sauce (page 191)
mint to garnish

**Serves 4**

## METHOD
Heat a lidded barbecue or oven to 320°F (160°C).

Cut into the skin of each banana by placing the banana flat on the chopping board and, with a small sharp knife, cut from a point ½ inch (1 cm) above the center point of the banana, all the way along the length of the banana to a point about 1 inch (2 cm) from the top, then curve the cut around and go down the banana again, leaving a parallel cut around an inch (2 cm) from the first cut and then, when you're about an inch (2 cm) from the tail end, turn the cut around again and slice back up almost to the point where you first started.

At this point you've made a long, oval door in the banana skin that will allow you to open up the banana once it's cooked.

Now place the bananas cut side up onto a tray lined with baking paper.

Place the tray on the barbecue or in the oven for 12–16 minutes or until the bananas are soft to touch.

When they're done, remove them from the heat and place them on to your serving plate.

Gently peel back the piece of skin you cut and extract the banana.

Serve with ice cream.

# » BANANA PANCAKES WITH MAPLE SAUCE

This is a great dessert or even a meal for brunch. Children particularly enjoy making pancakes.

## INGREDIENTS

6 oz (175 g) all purpose flour
2 teaspoons baking powder
¾ oz (20 g) brown sugar
1 pinch salt
2 eggs, lightly beaten
5½ fl oz (160 ml) milk
¾ fl oz. (20 ml) oil
2 bananas cut into ½ inch
 (1 cm) discs
canola oil, for cooking
Maple syrup

Makes 8–10 pancakes

## METHOD

To make the batter, mix the dry ingredients together in a medium-sized bowl.

Add the wet ingredients and mix well to form a smooth batter.

You can use the batter immediately but if you can, let the batter rest in the refrigerator for about half an hour for a better result. You can use this time to prepare plates, whip up some cream or cut fruit.

Using a flat top barbecue griddle or a non-stick frying pan on low-medium heat, drop a tablespoon of oil on the cooking surface and then evenly place about 3 or 4 tablespoons or half a ladle of mixture to form each small pancake.

Once you have placed the batter on to the cooking surface, place slices of banana onto the soft batter—around 4 pieces per pancake.

After 2–3 minutes (when the bottom of the pancake has turned golden brown and the top starts to become pitted) turn the pancake over and cook for a further 2–3 minutes or until the pancakes puff up.

Remove the pancakes from the pan and repeat the process until you've used up all the mixture.

Serve with maple syrup and freshly-sliced bananas or other fruit you might like.

# »ETON MESS (PF)

This is a great summer dessert to take on picnic or to a friend's house or to a family barbecue. It can be mostly made the previous day and put together just before leaving to ensure there is still some "crush" left in the meringues.

## INGREDIENTS
7 fl oz (200 ml) cream
1½ oz (40 g) icing sugar
9 oz (250 g) strawberry curd, lightly whisked
7 oz (200 g) pastry cream lightly whisked
10½ oz (300 g) fresh strawberries, calex removed and then quartered
reserve some to garnish
2¼ oz (60 g) meringues, crushed
mint, to garnish

**Serves 4**

## METHOD
In a large bowl, combine the cream and icing sugar. Whisk until firm.

Add the strawberry curd and pastry cream and gently fold together using a large spoon. The curd does not have to be totally mixed. This will give you a swirl effect.

Then add the fresh strawberries and meringues and gently fold these into the mixture.

Place mixture into a large serving bowl and garnish with the mint and some strawberries.

Serve within 1-2 hours or the meringues will go soft and lose their crunch.

# » GRILLED MANDARINS WITH ORANGE SAUCE & VANILLA ICE CREAM

Here is a great idea to use mandarins in a different way. They are very tasty warmed and it's another quick dessert for those that don't have a lot of time to spare. Fruit grilling is also a great way to utilize the barbecue for more than just the main meal.

## INGREDIENTS
8 easy peel mandarins
3½ fl oz (100 ml) water
8 teaspoons brown sugar
1 orange juice and zest
4½ oz (125 g) castor sugar
4 scoops vanilla ice cream of
  your choice
mint, to garnish

**Serves 4**

## METHOD
Peel the mandarins. Slice them in half along their "equator". Sprinkle their cut side with the brown sugar and allow them to stand for 5 minutes.

In a small pot bring the water, sugar and orange juice and zest to a boil then set aside.

Heat a barbecue griddle or pan to a low heat, then place the cut side of the mandarins onto the cooking surface. Leave them for 1–1.5 minutes until they brown lightly. Remove from the grill and serve with the orange syrup and vanilla ice cream to taste.

# » GRILLED PINEAPPLE WITH PASSIONFRUIT & TOFFEE SAUCE

Here is a great way to sweeten the end of any barbecue. The toffee sauce can be made in advance and the pineapples are quick to cook ensuring there is no long wait for dessert.

## INGREDIENTS

1 fresh whole pineapple peeled
  and cored cut into quarters
canola oil, and butter
4 halves passionfruit pulp
Mint leaves, to garnish
butter

### Toffee sauce

7 oz (200 g) brown sugar
6.76 fl oz (200 g) double cream
  (heavy)
1.78 oz (50 g) butter

**Serves 4**

## METHOD

Place all the ingredients for the toffee sauce in a medium-sized pot and bring to a boil.

Remove from the heat and whisk well. Store sauce in a clean airtight container in the fridge for up to 2 weeks.

Cut each pineapple quarter into 8 smaller pieces. First cut the quarter lengthways and then in halves and then half again lengthways.

Heat your clean, flat barbecue grill plate to a low–medium heat.

Add a little oil and once hot, and add the pineapple. Color to a dark gold evenly on two sides for 2–3 minutes each side.

Once colored, add a little butter and cook for a further minute.

Place the pineapple pieces on 4 separate plates with 8 pieces on each plate then cover the pineapple with the passionfruit pulp.

Liberally coat with toffee sauce and garnish with the mint.

Serve hot.

# » GRILLED PEACHES WITH ROAST PISTACHIO & WHIPPED ORANGE SCENTED CREAM

This dessert is wonderful when peach season has begun. It's an enjoyable way to eat peaches and it's quick to make for those who would like to spend more time relaxing in the evening sun.

## INGREDIENTS
4 large ripe peaches, halved
  and pitted
oil, for grilling
7 fl oz (200 ml) cream
1 oz (25 g) icing sugar
½ teaspoon orange zest

2¾ fl oz (80 ml) water
3½ oz (100 g) sugar
1 vanilla pod, split lengthwise
1 oz (30 g) pistachio nuts

Serves 4

## METHOD
In a medium size mixing bowl combine the cream, icing sugar and orange zest. Whisk until firm. Cover with plastic wrap and set aside in the refrigerator.

In a small pot bring the water, sugar and vanilla pod to a boil and set it aside.

Heat a barbecue grill or a grill pan to a medium-high heat.

Brush the peaches with a little oil and grill on the flat side until warmed and golden brown, then turn over to allow the underside to heat through.

Remove the peaches from heat, place them on serving tray and pour the warm sugar syrup over them.

Place spoonfuls of cream whipped with orange zest around the peaches, garnish with pistachio nuts and serve hot.

# » INDIVIDUAL TRIFLES (PF)

This is a great dessert to take to any picnic or outdoor party. They can be made the day before. Although the addition of sherry is one of the best things about these trifles, you'll have to hold back on it if the kids are going to be having some.

## INGREDIENTS
4½ oz (125 g) sugar
10 fl oz (300 ml) water
14 oz (400 g) fresh or frozen berries (raspberries, blackberries, strawberries)
6 leaves gelatine, soaked in cold water (or 12gm powdered gelatine)
3 oz (75 g) sponge cake diced into small cubes
1½ fl oz (40 ml) sherry
10½ oz (300 g) pastry cream
10½ oz (300 g) cream
¾ oz (20 g) icing sugar
mint, to garnish

**Serves 6**

## METHOD
To make the jelly, place the water and sugar in a medium-sized pot and over a high heat bring to a boil.

Once boiled, add the berries and remove from the heat. Allow to stand for 2 minutes then remove the berries and set these aside to cool.

Add the gelatine to the remaining liquid and dissolve it to make a jelly, then set it aside until close to the setting point.

Mix the sponge cake (and optional sherry) together, then mix in the cooled berries.

In six glasses place the sponge/berry (with optional sherry) mix in the bottom of the glass. Gently press down to get any air pockets out then pour over some of the cooled jelly liquid until it's just covering the sponge/berry mixture. Chill for 20 minutes.

After cooling, top the mixture with pastry cream forming an even flat layer which will "seal" in the sponge/berry/ jelly mix and prevent the next layer seeping through. Allow this to chill for 20 minutes in the refrigerator.

Then when the rest of the jelly mixture is close to setting, carefully pour it over the pastry cream, evenly spreading what you have between the six glasses. If you pour it slowly over the back of a spoon will prevent the jelly going through the pastry cream. Allow the glasses to set in the refrigerator for 1 hour or until the jelly is firm.

Whip the cream and icing sugar until it just holds its shape. Spoon this evenly over the top jelly layer in the six glasses and garnish the trifles with mint to serve.

# »LEMON TART (PF)

The perfect summer sweet treat that will finish any picnic with style, this is one of my favorite desserts and I often have one on the menu. The tarts always look beautiful either whole or cut. Serve with a little whipped cream and berries.

## INGREDIENTS

### Tart filling
12½ oz (350 g) sugar
9 eggs
7 fl oz (200 ml) lemon juice
5 fl oz (150 ml) cream
lemon zest from 2 of the
 leftover, juiced lemons

### Sweet pastry
8 oz (225 g) baker's flour
3½ oz (100 g) unsalted butter
 diced in small cubes
2 oz (50 g) icing sugar
1 small egg
pinch of salt
zest of half a lemon

Serves 6–8

## METHOD

To make the tart filling, in a small pot over a medium heat warm the cream and the zest to just below boiling point.

In a large bowl add the remaining ingredients and whisk together.

Strain the cream into the lemon/sugar mix and whisk.

Place the filling into a clean container ready for use. Set aside.

In a large bowl add the flour and butter and with your hands rub them together until you have a fine crumb without any lumps of butter. Do not overwork the pastry, you want this sand-like texture to start with.

Add the remaining ingredients and kneed only until you have formed a smooth dough.

Flatten the pastry out to form a disc of a diameter of about 6 inches (15 cm). Place the dough disc on a tray and cover it with plastic wrap and chill it in the refrigerator for about an hour.

Preheat the oven to 350°F (175°C).

Once the pastry is chilled, roll it to about 1/6 inch (3-4mm). Get a well-buttered 9-inch (23 cm) tart tin with a removable bottom. Now gently gather the pastry sheet and allow it to drop into the tin. Then gently press the pastry down into the tin pressing down gently onto the bottom and sides. Trim any excess pastry off.

Place the pastry-lined tin in the refrigerator for 30 minutes to let it rest.

After resting, line the uncooked pastry shell with baking paper and

recipe continues»

add rice, beans or ceramic baking beans and bake in the oven for 10-14 minutes until the pastry just starts to turn a little golden. This process is called "blind baking" because you're just baking the pastry without any filling in it.

Once the pastry shell is turning gold take it out of the oven and quickly remove the paper and rice or beans. Return the shell to the oven and then bake a further 10-12 minutes or until the pastry is a shade of deep gold.

Now remove the shell from the oven again and lower the temperature of the oven to 270°F (130°C).

Fill the tart shell with the lemon filling and bake the tart in the oven for 40-45 minutes or until the filling has set. The pastry should be a mid brown color when the tart is ready.

Once cooked, remove the tart and let it cool for a few minutes. You'll notice some shrinkage. At this point you should be able to remove the tart from the tin quite easily without risking breakage.

Allow the tart to cool on a wire rack and refrigerate it overnight.

When ready, serve with whipped cream and fresh berries.

# »RICH CHOCOLATE MOUSSE WITH RASPBERRIES (PF)

This is a real chocolate lover's dessert and it's easily transported. The mousse can be placed into cups and have the raspberries sprinkled on top to make little individual servings, which also look very pretty.

## INGREDIENTS

9 oz (250 g) dark chocolate 72–80 per cent cocoa (in buttons or cut into small pieces)
1½ oz (40 g) cocoa powder, sifted
10½ oz (300 g) cream
10 fl oz (300 ml) milk
3⅓ oz (90 g) sugar
4 egg yolks
½ teaspoon vanilla extract
raspberries, mint and cocoa powder, to garnish

**Serves 6**

## METHOD

Place the chocolate and cocoa powder into a medium-sized bowl and set aside.

In a medium-sized pot bring two cups of water to a boil. Once it reaches a boil place the chocolate mix bowl on top of the boiling water. Reduce the heat to low in order to melt the chocolate ensuring that no water makes contact with the chocolate.

In a separate medium-sized pot, heat the cream, milk and vanilla extract to a boil, then set it aside.

In a large bowl whisk the egg yolks and sugar together until they form a pale mix. Then, slowly add half the cream mix to the eggs and sugar while whisking continually.

Pour the mixture back into the pot that has the remaining cream and milk and place the pot over a medium heat and stir until it thickens to a thick, sauce-like consistency. Once thickened, pour into a clean bowl to stop further cooking.

Take the molten chocolate off the heat. Pour ¼ of the cream mixture into the chocolate mix and whisk until smooth, repeat this until well combined. Pour the chocolate mix into a clean bowl, cover and place it in the refrigerator to set.

To serve, use a heated spoon and form a quenelle, or an attractive smooth egg shape on the plate, and garnish with the raspberries and mint and dust with cocoa powder.

# CONDIMENTS & SAUCES

# »CHIPOTLE MAYONNAISE

This is a really tasty mayonnaise that can be used on many meats including burgers or larger fish cuts. If you don't want it too spicy just reduce the amount of chili you put in. I like a bit of spice so always add two.

## INGREDIENTS
2 egg yolks
1 tablespoon whole grain
  mustard
1 tablespoon white wine
  vinegar
3 cloves garlic, crushed
1–2 chipotle chilies, fresh or
  canned
1 teaspoon smoked paprika
7 fl oz (200 ml) canola oil
3–4 tablespoons water
salt and freshly-ground black
  pepper

Serves 8–10

## METHOD
In a food processer add the yolks, mustard, vinegar, smoked paprika, garlic and chilies.

Whisk well together and then while continually whisking slowly drizzle in the oil until you form an emulsion (a blended, thick liquid of mayonnaise-like consistency) ensuring that you use all of the oil.

Season to taste.

NOTE: Never add too much oil at once or the emulsion will "split" and the oil and water in the mixture will separate.

If the mixture it gets a little too thick add a very small amount of water to thin it down.

# »AIOLI

This simple garlic mayonnaise is a winner with seafood like squid, tuna and salmon. It will last well in the fridge and is always great to have on hand when you want a little more flavor or a sauce for barbecued foods.

## INGREDIENTS
2 egg yolks
1 tablespoon whole grain mustard
1 tablespoon white wine vinegar
7 fl oz (200 ml) canola oil
3 cloves crushed garlic
salt and freshly-ground black pepper to taste

## METHOD

In a medium bowl add the yolks, mustard, garlic and vinegar.

Whisk well together and then while continually whisking slowly drizzle in the oil until you form an emulsion (a blended, thick liquid of mayonnaise-like consistency), ensuring that you use all of the oil.

Season to taste.

NOTE: Never add too much oil at once or the emulsion will "split" and the oil and water in the mixture will separate.

If the mixture it gets a little too thick add a very small amount of water to thin it down.

# »CAFÉ DE PARIS BUTTER

This recipe does have quite a few ingredients but making this is really worth the time. It will keep frozen for months and it's always a very simple way to make any steak really tasty. It also goes very well on baked potatoes or grilled vegetables.

## INGREDIENTS
3½ oz (100 g) white onions,
   finely chopped
1 clove garlic, crushed
⅓ fl oz (10 ml) canola oil
½ fl oz (15 ml) white wine
1 pinch dried marjoram
1 pinch dried rosemary
1 pinch dried thyme
17½ oz (500 g) butter, softened
¼ teaspoon white pepper,
   ground
½ fl oz (15 ml) lemon juice
½ fl oz (15 ml) brandy
½ teaspoon curry powder
1 egg yolk
1 tablespoon smoked paprika
1 teaspoon salt
1 fl oz (10 ml)Worcestershire
   sauce
1½ fl oz (10 ml) madeira
1 tablespoon tomato paste
1 whole egg
1 teaspoon parsley, freshly
   chopped

## METHOD
In a medium pot, over a medium heat, add the oil and cook the onions and garlic until soft.

Add the white wine and dried herbs and cook until the wine has evaporated.

Cool to room temperature.

In a mixer with a paddle attachment, add the softened butter and beat on a medium speed until whitened, then add the all the other ingredients and mix at a slow speed.

Take a large piece of baking paper and place the butter mixture on the paper and roll it into a tube.

Set in the refrigerator and slice as needed.

NOTE: This will store for a few months in the freezer.

# » SMOKED BUTTER

I really like smoked butter. I often have it in the freezer. It's great tossed with fresh-steamed beans, topped on a perfectly cooked steak or with fresh boiled new potatoes. An excellent alternative to Café de Paris butter and just as versatile.

## INGREDIENTS
17½ oz (500 g) unsalted butter
salt

## METHOD

Cut the butter into four pieces and place two pieces in a bowl and set aside.

For smoking butter I like to use apple wood but use what you prefer and you will need enough wood or pallets in your smoker to achieve a 1.5 hour smoke (8 oz/ 250 g).

Cold smoke the butter for 1.5 hours ensuring the chamber temperature remains under 70°F (20°C) the entire time it is in the smoker. This is important as it's alright for the butter to soften but not for it to melt.

Lightly whip the 4 pieces of smoked butter together with a small electric mixer and season well with the salt to taste.

Take a large piece of baking paper and place the softened butter on the paper and roll it into a tube.

Set in the refrigerator and slice as needed.

NOTE: This butter will also store for a few months in the freezer.

I have found it best to smoke only half the butter and then to reintroduce the un-smoked half when seasoning. Lightly whip the smoked and unsmoked butter together or you might find the smoke is too overpowering in the final product.

# » BARBECUE SAUCE

This sauce can be used with barbecued ribs or mixed in with pulled pork but it's equally at home as a condiment with other barbecued meats like chicken and beef. I use it as I would tomato sauce or ketchup when having a barbecue.

## INGREDIENTS

8 fl oz (250 ml) tomato sauce or ketchup
4½ oz (125 g) liquid honey
4 fl oz (125 ml) cider vinegar
3 oz (75 g) mustard
1 brown onion diced
4 cloves garlic, crushed
2 chipotle chilies, dried or canned
¼ teaspoon celery seeds
2 tablespoons tabasco sauce
2 tablespoons Worcestershire sauce
8 fl oz (250 ml) tomato juice
2 tablespoons smoked paprika
salt and freshly-ground black pepper
canola oil, for cooking

## METHOD

In a large pot over a medium heat add the oil, then sauté the onions and garlic until soft. Add the celery seeds and chilies and cook for a further minute then add the remaining ingredients and bring to a boil.

Simmer until thickened, around 20 minutes.

Season and puree in a food processor until smooth.

Use immediately or store in an airtight container.

# »TOMATO CHUTNEY

A great addition to any picnic, this chutney will keep for 4-5 weeks in the refrigerator and can be used with a variety of different dishes, like burgers or as a sauce for steaks, as a picnic condiment or for barbecue chicken.

## INGREDIENTS
2¼ lb (1 kg) fresh, ripe tomatoes
5 Granny Smith apples, cored and diced
5 oz (150 g) brown sugar
4 fl oz (125 ml) red wine vinegar
4½ oz (125 g) raisins
2 brown onions, diced
1 green pepper (capscium), diced
1 teaspoon smoked paprika
salt and freshly-ground black pepper
Vegetable oil, for cooking

## METHOD
Heat a large pot over a medium heat, add a little vegetable oil, then sauté the onions until transparent. Add the apples and pepper and cook for a couple of minutes. To this add the remaining ingredients and cook over a low heat until the chutney thickens, usually about 1 hour and 15 minutes.

Remove from the heat and season well.

Store in jars or clean containers in the refrigerator.

NOTE: This chutney will keep for 6-8 weeks.

# »MINT SAUCE

This stylish sauce is a staple in my kitchen, it's so easy to prepare and goes great with lamb. I tried it first while in England, and have been using it ever since.

## INGREDIENTS
3 oz (75 g) fresh mint, retain 20 large leaves for garnish
5 fl oz (150 ml) red wine vinegar
5 oz (150 g) sugar

## METHOD
In a medium pot bring the red wine vinegar and sugar to a boil. Once boiled, set aside and add the mint and cool.

Once cool, strain the sauce into a serving container and a top with the fresh, finely-sliced mint.

# »VINAIGRETTE

This is a simple salad dressing that is white in color when it is ready. It can be kept in the fridge for 4–5 weeks and is my go-to salad dressing at home and in my kitchen.

## INGREDIENTS
1 tablespoon whole-grain mustard
1 tablespoon sugar
1 tablespoon salt
1¾ fl oz (50 ml) red wine vinegar
¼ teaspoon xanthan gum
7 fl oz (200 ml) canola oil
2½ fl oz (75 ml) water

## METHOD
Place the salt, whole-grain mustard, sugar, red wine vinegar and xanthan gum in a blender.

Start blending with the lid on then, remove the lid and start slowly pouring in the oil.

Once the mixture becomes thickened add some water to thin it out a little, then continue adding oil, then water, until you have incorporated it all.

Store in a airtight container in the refrigerator.

# »PICKLED RED ONIONS

## INGREDIENTS

16 oz (500 g) red onions, peeled and finely sliced
3 ½ fl oz (100 ml) white wine vinegar
4 ½ oz (125 g) castor sugar
1 cinnamon quill
3 whole cloves
1 chili, cut lengthways
¾ teaspoon salt

**Serves 4–6**

## METHOD

In a large saucepan place all the ingredients except the onions and bring to a boil, then add onions and simmer for 2–3 minutes. Remove when the onions are softened but still retain a little 'bite'.

Set aside to cool. Store in an airtight container in the fridge for up to 2 weeks. Remove the cinnamon, cloves and chili before serving.

# » CHILI CORN SALSA

This tasty fresh salsa goes well with chicken, fish and pork. It's best made an hour or so before needed to keep the ingredients crisp and fresh. For more heat, add chili to your taste.

## INGREDIENTS

1 corn cob grilled, corn kernels sliced from the cob
2 ripe tomatoes, deseeded and diced
1 small red onion, finely diced
3 tablespoons coriander, coarsely chopped
1 red chili, finely diced
1 spring onion, finely sliced
3 tablespoons red wine vinegar
3 tablespoons olive oil

Serves 4-6

## METHOD

Place all the ingredients into a medium-sized bowl and season well to taste.

Serve at room temperature.

# » YOGURT DRESSING

This simple yet tasty dressing pairs well with spiced foods like lamb koftas or spiced chicken. It is fresh-tasting and quick to prepare.

## INGREDIENTS

4 oz (125 g) natural yogurt
1 tbsp lemon juice
1 tbsp finely sliced fresh mint leaves
¼ cucumber, peeled and grated
salt and freshly ground pepper to taste

Serves 6–8

## METHOD

Mix all the ingredients together and season to taste.

# » MANGO & CHILI SALSA

This tasty and simple salsa is a great accompaniment to chicken and seafood alike, it's quick to make and adds bold color and flavor to your dish.

## INGREDIENTS

2 ripe mangoes, diced small
1 red onion, finely diced
1 red chili, de-seeded, finely diced
3 tablespoons coriander, finely chopped
3 tablespoons red wine vinegar
4 tablespoons extra-virgin olive oil
salt and freshly-ground black pepper

Serves 6–8

## METHOD

In a medium-sized bowl mix all the ingredients together and season to taste.

This can be kept for 3–4 days in the refrigerator but it's best served at room temperature.

# »CHOCOLATE SAUCE

This simple chocolate sauce recipe will keep in the fridge for 4-6 weeks and can be used with any dessert requiring chocolate sauce. It can be served warm or cold.

## INGREDIENTS

2 oz (60 g) unsweetened cocoa
   powder
6 fl oz (180m l) water
7 oz (200 g) white sugar

**Serves 12–15**

## METHOD

In a medium-sized pot add all the ingredients, place over a high heat and stir continuously until the mixture comes to a boil.

Remove from the heat and pour into a clean container.

Serve cold or warm.

# BRINES, RUBS, & OTHER BASICS

# » SALT WATER GLAZE

## INGREDIENTS
1 quart (1 liter) water
7 oz (200 g) salt
1–2 sprigs of rosemary

**Makes 1 cup**

## METHOD
In a medium-size pot, bring all the ingredients to a boil and leave to cool.

Strain and pour into a squeezable sauce bottle. Store at room temperature for up to 2 weeks.

# » BEEF MARINADE

## INGREDIENTS
4 cloves garlic, crushed
6 fl oz (175ml) canola oil
1 teaspoon freshly-ground black pepper
1 red chili, finely diced with seeds removed
1 tablespoon worcestershire sauce
1 tablespoon soy sauce
½ teaspoon smoked paprika

**Makes 1 cup**

## METHOD
Combine all the ingredients together and use as required. For storage place in an airtight container in the refrigerator for up to 1 month.

# »BEEF RUB #1

## INGREDIENTS
6 tablespoons flaky salt
3 tablespoons smoked paprika
4 tablespoons brown sugar
1 teaspoon freshly-ground black
  pepper
2 teaspoon cayenne pepper
1 teaspoon garlic powder
1 teaspoon onion powder
1 teaspoon dried basil

**Makes ¾ cup**

## METHOD
Combine all the ingredients and use as required. For storage, place in an airtight container for up to 1 month.

# »BEEF RUB #2

## INGREDIENTS
6 tablespoons flaky salt
1 tablespoon paprika
3 tablespoons brown sugar
2 teaspoon freshly-ground black
  pepper
1 teaspoon garlic powder
2 teaspoon onion powder
1 teaspoon dried sage
1 teaspoon oregano

**Makes ¾ cup**

## METHOD
Combine all the ingredients and use as required. For storage, place in an airtight container for up to 1 month.

# » CHICKEN RUB

## INGREDIENTS
3 tablespoons flaky salt
1 tablespoon white sugar
2 tablespoons smoked paprika
1 tablespoon dried thyme
1 tablespoon dried sage
1 teaspoon garlic powder

**Makes ½ cup**

## METHOD
Combine all the ingredients and use as required. For storage, place in an airtight container for up to 1 month.

# » CHICKEN BRINE

## INGREDIENTS
1 quart (1 liter) water
½ teaspoon celery seeds
2 tablespoons flaky salt
½ teaspoon ground white
  pepper
1½ tablespoon raw sugar
1 small fresh lime, halved

**Makes 1qt (1lt)**

## METHOD
In a medium pot place all the ingredients and bring to a boil. Chill and store in a clean airtight container until needed.

This brine will last 2-3 weeks in the refrigerator.

# »FISH BRINE #1

## INGREDIENTS
1 quart (1 liter) water
2 tablespoons salt

**Makes 1qt (1lt)**

## METHOD
In a medium pot bring 1 cup of water to a boil with the salt. Once dissolved add the remaining of the water and chill.

# »FISH BRINE #2

## INGREDIENTS
1 quart (1 liter) water
2 tablespoons salt
2 tablespoons sugar
1 lemon - zest and juice

**Makes 1qt (1lt)**

## METHOD
In a medium pot bring 1 cup of water to a boil with the salt, sugar and the zest and juice from one lemon. Once dissolved add the remaining water and chill.

# » LAMB RUB #1

## INGREDIENTS
6 tablespoons flaky salt
2 tablespoons smoked paprika
4 tablespoons brown sugar
1 teaspoon freshly-ground black
  pepper
2 teaspoon oregano dried
1 teaspoon basil dried
1 teaspoon onion powder

**Makes ¾ cup**

## METHOD
Combine all the ingredients and use as required. For storage, place in an airtight container for up to 1 month.

# » LAMB RUB #2

## INGREDIENTS
4 tablespoons flaky salt
1 tablespoon brown sugar
1 teaspoon thyme
1 teaspoon rosemary
1 tablespoon paprika
1 teaspoon garlic powder

**Makes ⅓ cup**

## METHOD
Combine all the ingredients and use as required. For storage, place in an airtight container for up to 1 month.

# » MEAT BRINE FOR BARBECUED MEATS

I use this brine for meats I plan on barbecuing or grilling, like pork loin, fillets or chops.

## INGREDIENTS
1 quart (1 liter) water
½ teaspoon celery seeds
12 peppercorns
½ teaspoon garlic powder
2 tablespoons flaky salt
1½ tablespoon brown sugar
1 small, fresh lime, halved

**Makes 1qt (1lt)**

## METHOD
In a medium pot place in all the ingredients and bring to a boil, chill and store in a clean airtight container until needed.

This brine will last 2-3 weeks in the refrigerator.

# » MEAT BRINE FOR SMOKED MEATS

I use this brine for all meats that I plan on smoking or pickling like corned beef, pickled pork or hams or bacon.

## INGREDIENTS

1 quart (1 liter) water
1 teaspoon colorquik
2 tablespoons table salt
1 tablespoon brown sugar
1 tablespoon honey
½ teaspoon garlic powder
16 pepper corns
1 teaspoon pickling spices

**Makes 1 qt (1 liter)**

## METHOD

In a medium pot place in all the ingredients and bring to a boil, chill and store in a clean airtight container until needed.

This brine will last 2-3 weeks in the refrigerator.

# INDEX

# GLOSSARY

**Back fat (pork):** raw, unrendered fat from between the muscle and the skin, available from your butcher. The best quality back fat is firm when cold, and very white in color.

**Brisket:** A cut that is taken from the breast section of beef or veal.

**Colorquik:** Also known as Prague powder or pink curing salt: the mix is dyed pink so as not to be confused with plain salt. It's a mix of around 94 per cent salt and 6 per cent nitrite. Colorquik is highly poisonous - check the instructions on the packet for safe handling of this product.

**Fat cap:** the layer of fat that lies between the muscle and the skin.

**Juniper berries:** the female seed cone produced from some species of junipers; they look like berries. They are used to give gin its flavor. Found in the spice section of the supermarket or gourmet food shop.

**Kalamata olives:** A type of black olive sourced from Greece.

**Kumara:** The New Zealand Maori name for the sweet potato.

**Manuka wood:** Sometimes known as Tea tree (Leptospermum scoparium). A myrtle tree native to New Zealand and South East Australia.

**Pickling spice:** A mix of spices usually containing a mix of, but not limited to, whole allspice, cilantro (coriander) seeds, whole peppercorns, whole cloves, small dried chilies and mustard seeds.

**Slider:** A sandwich served in a small bread bun.

**Snapper:** or Schnapper (Chrysophrys auratus). A large fish common in New Zealand coastal waters, elsewhere sometimes known as bream.

**Xanthan gum:** A polysaccharide secretion from bacteria used as a food additive. Commonly used as a thickening agent.

First published in 2016 by New Holland Publishers Pty Ltd

London · Sydney · Auckland

The Chandlery Unit 704 50 Westminster Bridge Road London SE1 7QY United Kingdom
1/66 Gibbes Street Chatswood NSW 2067 Australia
5/39 Woodside Ave Northcote, Auckland 0627 New Zealand

www.newhollandpublishers.com

A record of this book is held at the British Library, the National Library of Australia and
the National Library of New Zealand.

ISBN: 9781869664435

Managing Director: Fiona Schultz
Publisher: Christine Thomson
Project Editor: Xavier Waterkeyn
Photographer: Devin Hart
Production Director: James Mills-Hicks

Printer: Toppan Leefung Printing Ltd

10 9 8 7 6 5 4 3 2 1

Keep up with New Holland Publishers on Facebook www.facebook.com/NewHollandPublishers